EDINBURGH

TOP SIGHTS · LOCAL EXPERIENCES

NEIL WILSON

Contents

Plan Your Trip

Welcome to Edinburgh.......4

Top Sights............................6

Eating 10

Edinburgh on a Plate 12

Drinking..............................14

Edinburgh in a Glass.........16

Shopping............................18

Edinburgh Souvenirs.......20

Museums & Galleries 22

Festivals & Events............24

Architecture 26

Views 28

For Kids 29

Tours..................................30

Activities............................31

Four Perfect Days............32

Need to Know....................34

Edinburgh
Neighbourhoods..............36

Edinburgh Military Tattoo (p25)
DOMHNALL DODS/SHUTTERSTOCK ©

Explore Edinburgh   39

Old Town 41

Holyrood &
Arthur's Seat..................... 77

New Town........................... 91

West End &
Dean Village.................... 119

Stockbridge..................... 133

Leith................................. 147

South Edinburgh............. 161

Worth a Trip

Rosslyn Chapel 174

Survival Guide   177

Before You Go 178

Arriving in Edinburgh 179

Getting Around 180

Essential Information 181

Index................................ 186

Special Features

Edinburgh Castle 42

National Museum
of Scotland......................... 48

Palace of
Holyroodhouse................... 78

Scottish
Parliament Building...........80

Royal Yacht Britannia......148

COVID-19

We have re-checked every business in this book before publication to ensure that it is still open after 2020's COVID-19 outbreak. However, the economic and social impacts of COVID-19 will continue to be felt long after the outbreak has been contained, and many businesses, services and events referenced in this guide may experience ongoing restrictions. Some businesses may be temporarily closed, have changed their opening hours and services, or require bookings; some unfortunately could have closed permanently. We suggest you check with venues before visiting for the latest information.

Welcome to Edinburgh

Edinburgh is one of Britain's most beautiful and dramatic cities, with its castle perched on the summit of ancient crags and the medieval maze of the Old Town gazing across verdant gardens to the elegant Georgian squares and streetscapes of the New Town. History and architecture are leavened with a bacchanalia of bars, innovative restaurants and Scotland's most stylish shops.

Princes Street (p18)

Top Sights

MARCANDRELLETOURNEUX/SHUTTERSTOCK ©

Edinburgh Castle

Scotland's most popular tourist attraction. **p42**

Real Mary King's Close

Lost world beneath the streets. **p46**

National Museum of Scotland

Treasure house of Scottish culture. **p48**

Palace of Holyroodhouse

The Queen's Edinburgh residence. **p78**

Scottish Parliament Building

Visual feast of modern architecture. **p80**

Scottish National Portrait Gallery

Visual encyclopedia of famous Scots. **p92**

Princes Street Gardens

Green oasis in the city centre. **p94**

Scottish National Gallery of Modern Art

Masterpieces of contemporary art. **p120**

Royal Botanic Garden

Tranquil haven of lush greenery. **p134**

Royal Yacht Britannia

Royal family's floating palace. **p148**

Rosslyn Chapel

Medieval mystery carved in stone. **p174**

Eating

Eating out in Edinburgh has changed beyond all recognition since the 1990s. Back then, sophisticated dining meant a visit to the Aberdeen Angus Steak House for a prawn cocktail, steak (well done) and chips, and Black Forest gateau. Today, central Edinburgh has more restaurants per head of population than any other UK city, including a handful of places with Michelin stars.

Modern Scottish Cuisine

Scotland has never been celebrated for its national cuisine – in fact, with popular dishes ranging from haggis and porridge to deep-fried Mars bars, it has more often been an object of ridicule. But since the early 2000s chefs have been taking top-quality Scottish produce – from Highland venison, Aberdeen Angus beef and freshly landed seafood to root vegetables, raspberries and regional cheeses – and preparing it simply, in a way that emphasises the natural flavours, often adding a French, Italian or Asian twist.

Haggis – Scotland's National Dish

The raw ingredients of Scotland's national dish (pictured) don't sound too promising – the finely chopped lungs, heart and liver of a sheep, mixed with oatmeal and onion and stuffed into a sheep's stomach bag. However, it tastes surprisingly good and is on the menu in many restaurants, whether served with the traditional accompaniment of mashed potatoes and turnip, or given a modern twist such as haggis in filo pastry parcels with hoisin sauce.

Best Modern Scottish

Condita Michelin-starred perfection from this South-side newcomer. (p166)

Timberyard Seasonally changing menu sourced from artisan growers and foragers. (p123)

Outlook The best of Scottish produce served with a stunning view. (p105)

PAUL_BRIGHTON/SHUTTERSTOCK ©

Best Traditional Scottish

Amber Set in the Scotch Whisky Experience; many dishes include whisky in the recipe. (p67)

McKirdy's Steakhouse Prime Scottish beef, simply prepared and served in a friendly setting. (p124)

Witchery by the Castle Wonderfully over-the-top Gothic decor, great steak and seafood, and fine wines. (p66)

Cannonball Classic haggis, steak and lobster dishes within sight of the castle. (p63)

Best Seafood

Ondine Beautiful dining room, with a menu based on sustainably sourced fish. (p63)

Fishers Bistro A local institution, with North Berwick lobster a speciality. (p154)

Fishmarket Harbourside restaurant and takeaway serving the city's best fish and chips. (p153)

Best Vegetarian

David Bann Smart and sophisticated, bringing an inventive approach to vegetarian food. (p67)

Kalpna Long-established Indian restaurant, famous for its all-you-can-eat lunch buffet. (p168)

Holy Cow Great-value vegetarian fare, including their famous vegan burgers. (p110)

Foodie Tips

o Book well in advance for top restaurants

o The *Edinburgh & Glasgow Eating & Drinking Guide* (http://food.list.co.uk) has restaurant, cafe and bar reviews.

o Check www.5pm.co.uk for restaurants with tables to spare that evening.

Edinburgh on a Plate
Cullen Skink

Boiled potatoes are added to the milk and onions, and the cooked fish is flaked in last.

The onions are chopped and softened in butter, then the fish-infused milk is added.

Variations include using leeks instead of onion, cream instead of milk, and adding herbs.

The smoked haddock is poached gently in the milk to make the base for the soup, then removed.

★ Top Places for Cullen Skink

Scottish Cafe & Restaurant (p110) This appealing modern restaurant has picture windows providing a view along Princes Street Gardens.

Amber (p67) This whisky-themed restaurant creates genuinely interesting and flavoursome dishes using top Scottish produce, with a suggested whisky pairing for each dish.

Museum Brasserie (p49) The restaurant in the Victorian part of the National Museum of Scotland serves tasty light lunches, including Scottish-beef burger, fish and chips, and specials such as venison sausages with red-onion gravy.

No 1 The Grange (p167) The menu at this friendly neighbourhood gastropub revolves around a cluster of crowd-pleasing classics.

Cullen Skink Essentials

Named for the old fishing harbour of Cullen on Scotland's northeast coast, and from the old Scots word 'skink' (soup), Cullen skink is a delicious, warming broth made with smoked haddock, potatoes, onion, butter and milk, usually served with crusty bread and butter. Originally a regional speciality, since the 1990s it has become ubiquitous in Edinburgh restaurants, and many places have spruced up the old recipe with the addition of cream, leeks, white wine and herbs.

Cullen Skink

Drinking

Edinburgh has always been a drinkers' city. It has more than 700 pubs – more per square mile than any other UK city – and they are as varied and full of character as the people who drink in them. From Victorian palaces to stylish pre-club bars, and from real-ale howffs (meeting places, often pubs) to cool cocktail lounges there's a bar to please every taste.

WILL SALTER/LONELY PLANET ©

Edinburgh Beers

By the end of the 19th century, Edinburgh ranked alongside Munich, Pilsen and Burton-on-Trent in importance as a brewing centre, with no fewer than 35 breweries. Today the city's two large-scale breweries – Caledonian (creator of Deuchars IPA) and Stewart Brewing (producer of Edinburgh Gold) – have been joined by an ever-growing number of microbreweries and brewpubs.

Trad vs Trendy

At one end of Edinburgh's spectrum of hostelries lies the traditional 19th-century pub, which has preserved much of its original Victorian decoration and generally serves real ales, craft beers and a range of malt whiskies. At the other end is the modern cocktail bar, with a cool clientele and sharp styling.

Opening Times

Pubs generally open from 11am to 11pm Monday to Saturday and 12.30pm to 11pm on Sunday. Many open later on Friday and Saturday, closing at midnight or 1am, while some with a music licence party on until 3am.

Best Historic Pubs

Bennet's Bar Locals pub (pictured above) with lovely Victorian fittings. (p170)

Café Royal Circle Bar City-centre haven of Victorian splendour, famed for Doulton ceramic portraits. (p111)

Sheep Heid Inn Semi-rural retreat in the shadow of Arthur's Seat, famed as Edinburgh's oldest pub. (p88)

Guildford Arms A time capsule of polished mahogany and gleaming brass. (p112)

T.W. VAN URK/SHUTTERSTOCK ©

Best Craft-Beer Pubs

Brauhaus Tiny bar with a huge selection of beers from all over the world. (p170)

Blue Blazer Resolutely old-fashioned pub with a good range of Scottish ales. (p127)

Auld Hoose Great jukebox plus a broad range of beers from Scottish microbreweries. (p170)

Best Cocktail Bars

Bramble Possibly the city's best cocktails, served in an atmospheric cellar bar. (p112)

Tigerlily Cocktails as colourful as the swirling, glittering designer decor. (p113)

Lucky Liquor Co Tiny but highly rated bar serving inventive and unusual cocktails. (p111)

Best Whisky Bars

Bow Bar Busy Grassmarket-area pub with a huge selection of malt whiskies. (p68)

Malt Shovel Old-school pub (pictured above) with more than 100 single malts behind the bar. (p71)

Last Word Saloon Small but well-chosen selection; good place to dip a toe in the world of whisky. (p141)

Gigs & Crowds

● The Gig Guide (www.gigguide.co.uk) is a monthly email newsletter and listings website covering pub live music.

● To avoid Friday and Saturday night crowds, steer clear of the Grassmarket, the Cowgate and Lothian Rd.

Edinburgh in a Glass

Whisky

One part spring water

Two parts single malt whisky

★ Where to Learn About Whisky

Scotch Whisky Experience (p58) Interactive multimedia attraction that explains the whole process of making Scotland's national drink.

Holyrood Distillery (p87) Take a tour of the city's first working distillery since 1925.

Royal Mile Whiskies (p73) The knowledgeable staff at this long-established shop will help you choose a bottle to remember.

Whisky in Edinburgh

Whisky is, of course, the quintessentially Scottish drink, made with malted barley, water and yeast. Until the opening of the Holyrood Distillery in 2019, there had not been any distilleries in operation in Edinburgh since 1925. But the city's port of Leith was once a centre of the whisky industry, with a dozen working distilleries and acres of bonded warehouses where the spirit was stored and matured.

Scotch single malts

Shopping

Edinburgh's shopping experience extends far beyond the big-name department stores of Princes St, ranging from designer fashion and handmade jewellery to independent bookshops, delicatessens and farmers markets. Classic north-of-the-border buys include cashmere, Harris tweed, tartan goods, Celtic jewellery and Scotch whisky.

Princes Street

Princes St is Edinburgh's trademark shopping strip, lined with big high-street names including Marks & Spencer, Debenhams and the Apple Store. There are more designer boutiques a block north on George St, and smaller specialist stores on Rose and Thistle Sts. There are also two big city-centre shopping malls – Princes Mall, at the eastern end of Princes St, and the new St James Quarter (scheduled to open in 2021), at the top of Leith St – plus Multrees Walk, a designer shopping complex with Harvey Nichols on the eastern side of St Andrew Sq.

Shopping Districts

Other central shopping streets include South Bridge, Nicolson St and Lothian Rd. For more offbeat shopping – including fashion, music, crafts and jewellery – head for Cockburn, Victoria and St Mary's Sts, all leading off the Royal Mile; William St (West End); and Raeburn Pl and St Stephen's St (Stockbridge). Ocean Terminal (Leith) is another huge mall.

Best Department Stores

Jenners An Edinburgh shopping institution, with a wide range of quality goods. (p117)

Harvey Nichols Four floors of designer labels and eye-popping price tags. (p117)

John Lewis Classic British store with a focus on quality goods and service. (p117)

Best for Tartan

Kinloch Anderson Tailors and kiltmakers for the royal family. (p158)

Geoffrey (Tailor) Inc Kilts in all patterns, from clan

CHRISTIAN MUELLER/SHUTTERSTOCK ©

tartans to football colours. (p74)

Jenners Browse goods made in tartan and tweed in the Great Hall. (p117)

Best Markets

Edinburgh Farmers Market Saturday feast of fresh Scottish produce (p127; pictured).

Stockbridge Market Eclectic Sunday market that's become a focus for the local community. (p143)

Pitt Weekly street-food market. (p155)

Best for Jewellery

Galerie Mirages Best known for silver, amber and gemstone jewellery in traditional and contemporary designs. (p145)

Alchemia Original designs plus specially commissioned pieces. (p116)

Annie Smith Edinburgh designer famed for beautiful and delicate pieces reflecting nature's patterns. (p144)

Best for Books

Lighthouse Radical bookshop specialising in political, gay and feminist literature. (p173)

McNaughtan's Bookshop Secondhand and antiquarian dealer with books on Scottish history, art and architecture. (p116)

Golden Hare Voted UK Independent Bookshop of the Year in 2019. (p143)

Shopping for Tips

○ From 1 January 2021 visitors from both EU and non-EU countries can no longer claim back VAT (value-added tax) on purchased goods.

○ Many city-centre shops stay open till 7pm or 8pm on Thursday.

Edinburgh Souvenirs

NATALIYA HORA/SHUTTERSTOCK ©

Scotch Whisky

Track down that single malt you really enjoyed at Royal Mile Whiskies (p73) – the staff know all there is to know about Scotch whisky.

Tartan Goods

It might seem a bit old-fashioned, but tartan is back on trend. Pick up scarves, bags and other tartan accessories at Jenners (p117).

TAMUT/SHUTTERSTOCK ©

Cashmere

Scotland has a long-standing reputation for producing high-quality cashmere goods. Head to Harvey Nichols (p117) for luxurious scarves from Johnstons of Elgin.

Harris Tweed

With colours that reflect the heather and heath of the Scottish hills, tweed fabric has hit the fashion heights; Ragamuffin (p73) has a superb selection.

Celtic Jewellery

Perre (p116) stocks silver earrings, necklaces and brooches with intricate Celtic knot designs inspired by the patterns carved on ancient Scottish stones.

Museums & Galleries

As Scotland's capital city, it's hardly surprising that Edinburgh is home to some of the country's most important museums and art collections. Admire the Old Masters, from Titian to Turner, at the Scottish National Gallery; hone your knowledge of Scottish heritage at the National Museum of Scotland or delve into the arcane delights of the city's lesser-known collections.

Special Events

Several of the city's major institutions host special events and after-hours visits. The National Museum of Scotland stages Museum After Hours events throughout the year, with live music, lectures and behind-the-scenes tours, while the National Gallery of Scotland and the National Portrait Gallery stage musical performances, educational talks and art lessons. Check the museum's website What's On or Events links for details.

Admission & Access

National collections (eg National Museum of Scotland, Scottish National Gallery, Scottish National Portrait Gallery, Scottish National Gallery of Modern Art) and Edinburgh city-owned museums (Museum of Edinburgh, City Art Centre etc) have free admission, except for temporary exhibitions where a fee is often charged. Most private galleries are also free; smaller museums often charge an entrance fee, typically around £5 (book online at some museums for discounted tickets). National collections are generally open from 10am to 5pm, with the Scottish National Gallery staying open till 7pm on Thursday.

Best Collections

National Museum of Scotland Beautiful setting for collections covering Scottish history, the natural world, art and engineering. (p48)

Scottish National Portrait Gallery Far more interesting than the name implies, especially after a recent revamp. (p92)

CLIVEWA/SHUTTERSTOCK ©

Scottish National Gallery Old masters, Scottish artists, and Canova's famous marble sculpture of the Three Graces. (p102)

Scottish National Gallery of Modern Art Pride of place goes to works by the Scottish Colourists, Eduardo Paolozzi and Barbara Hepworth. (p120)

Best Smaller Museums

Museum of Edinburgh The city: Stone Age to the present. (p58)

Surgeons' Hall Museums Grisly but fascinating collection on the history of surgery. (p164)

Writers' Museum All you ever wanted to know about Robert Burns, Walter Scott

and Robert Louis Stevenson. (p59)

Best Museum Architecture

Scottish National Portrait Gallery Gorgeous palace (pictured above) in Venetian Gothic style, studded with sculptures of famous Scots. (p92)

National Museum of Scotland Staid Victorian building set off by flamboyant modern extension in golden sandstone. (p48)

Museum of Edinburgh Set in a 16th-century house with colourful, ornate decoration in red and yellow ochre. (p58)

Art Tours & Meals

∘ The national collections have useful 'trail' leaflets that guide you around their highlights.

∘ All major museums and galleries have good restaurants or cafes, often worth a visit in their own right.

Festivals & Events

Edinburgh is one of the world's biggest party venues, with a crowded calendar of festivals ranging from science to movies and military bands. High season is August, when half a dozen festivals, including the Edinburgh International Festival and Festival Fringe, run concurrently. It's followed by the Christmas festival and Hogmanay celebrations.

Edinburgh International Festival

First held in 1947 to mark a return to peace after the ordeal of WWII, the Edinburgh International Festival is festooned with superlatives – the oldest, the biggest, the most famous, the best in the world. The festival occurs over the three weeks ending on the first Saturday in September; the program is usually available from April. Tickets sell out quickly, so it's best to book as far in advance as possible.

Edinburgh Festival Fringe

When the first Edinburgh International Festival was held, eight theatre companies didn't make it onto the main programme. Undeterred, they grouped together and held their own mini-festival, on the fringe, and an Edinburgh institution was born. The Fringe takes place over 3½ weeks, the last two overlapping with the first two of the Edinburgh International Festival.

Big-name tickets can cost £15 to £20 and up, but there are plenty of good shows in the £5 to £15 range and lots of free stuff.

Best Festivals

Edinburgh International Science Festival (April) Hosts a wide range of events, including talks, lectures, exhibitions, demonstrations and guided tours designed to stimulate, inspire and challenge.

Imaginate Festival (May) Britain's biggest festival of performing arts for children (for kids aged three to 12). Groups from around the world perform classic tales like *Hansel and Gretel*, and new material written specially for children.

Edinburgh International Film Festival (June) The two-week film festival is a

JAN KRANENDONK/SHUTTERSTOCK ©

major international event, serving as a showcase for new British and European films and for the European premieres of some Hollywood blockbusters.

Edinburgh International Festival (August) Hundreds of the world's top musicians and performers congregate for three weeks of diverse and inspirational music, opera, theatre and dance.

Edinburgh Festival Fringe (August) The biggest festival of the performing arts in the world (pictured).

Edinburgh Military Tattoo (August) A spectacular display of military marching bands, massed pipes and drums, acrobats, cheerleaders and more, with the magnificent backdrop of the floodlit castle.

Edinburgh International Book Festival (August) A fun fortnight of talks, readings, debates, lectures, book signings and meet-the author events.

Best Events

Beltane (April/May) A pagan fire festival marking the end of winter, celebrated on Calton Hill's summit.

Royal Highland Show (late June) A four-day feast of all things rural, from tractor driving to sheep shearing.

Edinburgh's Christmas (December) Includes a street parade, fairground and Ferris wheel, and an open-air ice rink in Princes Street Gardens.

Edinburgh's Hogmanay (29 December to 1 January) Events include a torchlight procession and huge street party.

Gig Listings

The List (www.list.co.uk) is an excellent, comprehensive free listings website and magazine covering what's on in Edinburgh and Glasgow. Published every two months, it's available from most newsagents.

Architecture

Edinburgh's unique beauty arises from a combination of its unusual site, perched among craggy hills, and fine architecture, dating from the 16th century to the present. The New Town remains the world's most complete and unspoilt example of Georgian architecture. Along with the Old Town, it was declared a Unesco World Heritage Site in 1995.

Old Town Tenements

Edinburgh's Old Town features Britain's biggest concentration of surviving 17th-century buildings. These tenements were among the tallest in Britain in their time. You can explore them at Gladstone's Land (p59) and John Knox House (p60).

Georgian Gorgeousness

Robert Adam (1728–92), one of the Georgian period's leading architects, made his mark with neoclassical masterpieces such as Charlotte Sq (p102) and Edinburgh University's Old College. The Georgian House (p102) displays the elegance of Adam's interiors.

Modern Masterpiece

New Town's plan was the result of a competition won by James Craig, an unknown, self-taught architect. Another competition saw Enric Miralles chosen as the architect for the Scottish Parliament Building (p80). Though it was controversial, the prize-winning building revitalised a near-derelict industrial site on the Royal Mile.

Best Modern Architecture

Scottish Parliament Building Ambitious and controversial: Scotland's most exciting example of modern architecture (p80; pictured)

National Museum of Scotland Its golden sandstone lines create echoes of castles, churches, gardens and cliffs. (p48)

Scottish Poetry Library Cleverly insinuated into a cramped space in an Old Town alley. (p87)

ARCHITECT: ENRIC MIRALLES; BRENDAN HOWARD/SHUTTERSTOCK ©

Front Range The Royal Botanic Garden's designer glasshouses are included in *Prospect* magazine's Top 100 Modern Scottish Buildings. (p134)

Best Neoclassical Architecture

Charlotte Sq The Adam facade on its north side is the jewel in the New Town's architectural crown. (p102)

Royal Scottish Academy Imposing Doric temple dominating Princes St's centre. (p102)

Dundas House Gorgeous Palladian mansion that's now a bank; pop into the main hall to view the spectacular dome. (p104)

Best Early Architecture

Parliament Hall This grandiose 17th-century hall has a majestic hammer-beam roof, and was once home to the Scottish Parliament. (p63)

Best Monuments

Scott Monument This Gothic space rocket in Princes Street Gardens celebrates the famous

historical novelist Sir Walter Scott. (p95)

Nelson Monument This slender tower on Calton Hill's summit was built to commemorate Nelson's victory at Trafalgar in 1805. (p103)

National Monument An unfinished folly atop Calton Hill; its Greek-temple-like appearance gave Edinburgh the nickname 'Athens of the North'. (p104)

Architecture Online

⊙ The website www.edinburgharchitecture. co.uk provides useful info, including on special events and guided architectural walking tours.

Views

Edinburgh is one of Europe's most beautiful cities, draped across rocky hills overlooking the sea. A glance at any souvenir shop's postcards reveals the city's many viewpoints. Part of the pleasure of any visit to Edinburgh is simply soaking up the scenery, so set aside some time to explore the loftier parts of the city.

JONATHAN SMITH/LONELY PLANET ©

Best Natural Viewpoints

Arthur's Seat Sweeping panoramas from the highest point in Edinburgh. (p85; pictured)

Calton Hill Edinburgh's templed 'acropolis' affords a superb view along Princes St. (p103)

Blackford Hill This craggy eminence provides a grandstand view of Castle Rock and Arthur's Seat. (p166)

Royal Botanic Garden Set on a rise to the north of the city centre, with a grand view back towards the castle perched on its crag. (p134)

Best Architectural Viewpoints

Scott Monument Climb 287 steps to the top of this Gothic pinnacle, and look out over Princes Street Gardens. (p95)

Camera Obscura The Outlook Tower here provides an iconic view along the Royal Mile. (p58)

Castle Esplanade Commanding views north across the New Town, or south towards the Pentland Hills.

National Museum of Scotland Take the lift to the roof terrace and enjoy a fantastic view across the city to the castle ramparts. (p48)

Best Restaurant Views

Outlook Perched at the top of Calton Hill, with a superb view across the city. (p105)

Maxie's Bistro Outdoor tables on the terrace look out over Victoria St to the Grassmarket. (p68)

Scottish Cafe & Restaurant The window tables here have a lovely outlook along Princes Street Gardens. (p110)

Fishmarket Outdoor terrace tables offer a view across Newhaven harbour to the Forth Bridges. (p153)

Royal Deck Tea Room The sun deck on the Royal Yacht *Britannia* enjoys a vista over the Firth of Forth and the hills of Fife. (p149)

For Kids

LOU ARMOR/SHUTTERSTOCK ©

Edinburgh has plenty of attractions for children, and most things to see and do are child friendly. During the Edinburgh and Fringe Festivals there's lots of street theatre for kids, especially on High St and at the foot of the Mound, and in December there's a Ferris wheel and fairground rides in Princes Street Gardens and an ice rink in St Andrew Sq.

Best Sights for Kids

Edinburgh Castle Ask at the ticket office about the Children's Quiz, which lets kids track down various clues and treasures. (p42)

Edinburgh Zoo Giant pandas, interactive chimpanzee enclosure, penguins on parade. (p105; pictured)

Our Dynamic Earth Loads of great stuff, from earthquake simulators to real icebergs. (p86)

Camera Obscura Fascinating exhibits on illusions, magic tricks, electricity and holograms. (p58)

Real Mary King's Close Older children will enjoy the ghost stories and creepy atmosphere here.

Children under five years not admitted. (p46)

Scott Monument Lots of narrow stairs to climb, grotesque carvings to spot and a view at the top. (p95)

Royal Yacht Britannia Kids will love exploring the various decks, control rooms and engine rooms. (p148)

Best Museums for Kids

National Museum of Scotland Lots of interactive exhibits, and trail leaflets for kids to follow and fill in. (p48)

Scottish National Gallery of Modern Art Great landscaped grounds for exploring – track down all the sculptures! (p120)

Travel with Little Ones

○ *Edinburgh for Under Fives* (www.efuf.co.uk) has a useful website and guidebook. See also www.list.co.uk/kids.

○ Two kids under five can travel free on public transport with a fare-paying adult; kids five to 15 pay half the adult fare.

Tours

JAUME/SHUTTERSTOCK ©

Best Walking Tours

City of the Dead Tours
(📞0131-225 9044; www.cityofthedeadtours.com; 26a Candlemaker Row, EH1 2QE; adult/concession £14/10; ⏰9pm Easter-Oct, 8.30pm Tue & Thu-Sat Nov-Easter) This tour of Greyfriars Kirkyard is probably the scariest of Edinburgh's 'ghost' tours.

Edinburgh Literary Pub Tour
(www.edinburghliterarypubtour.co.uk; Beehive Inn, Grassmarket, EH1 2JU; adult/student £16/14; ⏰7.30pm daily May-Sep, limited days Oct-Apr) A two-hour trawl through Edinburgh's literary history and associated howffs.

Mercat Tours
(📞0131-225 5445; www.mercattours.com; Mercat Cross, EH1 1RF; adult/child £16/11; ⏰10am-9.30pm; 🚌35) Offers fascinating history walks and 'Ghosts & Ghouls' tours.

Cadies & Witchery Tours
(📞0131-225 6745; www.witcherytours.com; 84 West Bow, EH1 2HH; adult/child £10/7.50; ⏰7pm year-round, plus 9pm Apr-Sep; 🚌2) Murder & Mystery tours of the Old Town's darker corners, with 'jumperooters' – costumed actors who 'jump oot' unexpectedly.

Rebus Tours
(📞0131-553 7473; www.rebustours.com; Royal Oak, Infirmary St, EH1 1LT; per person £20; ⏰noon Sat) Tours of the 'hidden Edinburgh' frequented by novelist Ian Rankin's detective, John Rebus.

Invisible (Edinburgh)
(📞07500-773709; www.invisible-cities.org/cities/edinburgh; per person from £12) This venture trains homeless people as tour guides: themes include Crime & Punishment and Powerful Women.

Best Bus Tour

Majestic Tour
(www.edinburghtour.com/majestic-tour; St Andrew Sq, EH2 1BB; adult/child £16/free; ⏰daily year-round except 25 Dec) Hop-on, hop-off tour departing every 15 to 20 minutes from St Andrew Sq to the Royal Yacht *Britannia* via the New Town, the Royal Botanic Garden and Newhaven, returning via Leith Walk, Holyrood and the Royal Mile.

Best Boat Tour

3 Bridges Tour
(www.edinburghtour.com/3-bridges-tour; adult/child £25/12; ⏰departs 10am & noon Fri-Sun) This half-day tour begins with a bus from St Andrew Sq to South Queensferry, where you board a boat for a tour beneath the three bridges spanning the Firth of Forth, before going seal-spotting at Inchcolm Island.

Activities

AEYPIX/SHUTTERSTOCK ©

Edinburgh has plenty of places to perk up your sagging muscles with a spot of healthy exercise. Hikers can head for the Holyrood Park or Hermitage of Braid, cyclists can take advantage of the city's network of cycle paths, and golfers can take their pick from around 90 courses within easy reach of the city.

Best for Walking

Arthur's Seat Hike to the summit for outstanding views (pictured above). (p85)

Holyrood Park Jog around Arthur's Seat through this little bit of wilderness in the heart of the city. (p86)

Hermitage of Braid Enjoy a rural walk along this lovely wooded glen. (p166)

Best for Cycling

Water of Leith Walkway (www.wateofleith.org.uk/walkway) Runs from the sea at Leith to the Pentland Hills southwest of the city.

Innocent Railway A dedicated cycle path running from the southern side of Arthur's Seat eastwards to Musselburgh (5 miles) and on to Ormiston and Pencaitland.

Best for Golfing

Leith Links Visit the place where the rules of golf were formalised in 1744. (p151)

Activities Information

○ The **Scottish Rights of Way & Access Society** (☏0131-558 1222; www.scotways.com) provides information and advice on walking trails and rights of way.

○ Check out www.scottishgolfcourses.com for details of Edinburgh's golf courses.

○ A variety of bikes can be rented from **Biketrax** (p181).

Four Perfect Days

Day 1

Spend the first two hours of the morning at **Edinburgh Castle** (p42), then stroll down the Royal Mile, stopping off for a pre-booked tour of the historic **Real Mary King's Close** (p46).

At the bottom of the Mile, take a one-hour guided tour of the **Scottish Parliament Building** (p80), before crossing the street to the **Palace of Holyrood-house** (p78). Then, if the weather's fine, head up the stairs from nearby Calton Rd to the summit of **Calton Hill** (p103) for superb views across the city.

Before or after dinner, scare yourself silly on a ghost tour of **Greyfriars Kirkyard** (p60; pictured), then head to the **Bongo Club** (p69) or **Cabaret Voltaire** (p68) for some alternative-style entertainment.

Day 2

Make morning number two a feast of culture, with a tour of the **National Museum of Scotland** (p48; pictured), followed by a stroll down the Mound to the **Scottish National Gallery** (p102).

Climb to the top of the **Scott Monument** (p95) for panoramic views, then catch a bus from Princes St to Ocean Terminal for a visit to the **Royal Yacht Britannia** (p148). Time your trip to get the last two hours of opening here.

Stay in Leith for a pint at **Teuchters Landing** (p158) or a cocktail in a teapot at the **Roseleaf** (p157), or head back to the city centre to sample some Edinburgh-brewed beer in the magnificent surroundings of the **Café Royal Circle Bar** (p111).

Day 3

GEORGECLERK/GETTY IMAGES ©

Day 4

IORDANIS/SHUTTERSTOCK ©

Begin with a visit to the **Scottish National Gallery of Modern Art** (p120), then walk along the Water of Leith Walkway to Stockbridge and explore the boutiques on St Stephen St before pausing for lunch.

If it's Sunday, browse the stalls at **Stockbridge Market** (p143; pictured), then make the short stroll to the **Royal Botanic Garden** (p134). This is one of the UK's leading gardens, so devote the rest of the afternoon to exploring the palm houses, rock gardens, woodland gardens and outdoor sculptures.

Have tickets booked for a show at the **Royal Lyceum** (p129) or the **Traverse** (p129), or else head for late-night traditional Scottish music and dancing at **Ghillie Dhu** (p128).

Head to the southern fringes of the city and devote the morning to the *Da Vinci Code* delights of **Rosslyn Chapel** (p174). This 15th-century church is a monument to the stonemason's art.

Return to the city centre to spend the afternoon browsing the New Town shops and visiting the **Scottish National Portrait Gallery** (p92), which leads you through Scottish history via portraits of famous personalities. Take an early-evening stroll through **Princes Street Gardens** (p94; pictured), then wander down Leith Walk to **Joseph Pearce's** (p111) for a gin and tonic before dinner.

Round off the evening with some live jazz at the **Jazz Bar** (p72), or a comedy act at **The Stand** (p113).

Need to Know

For detailed information, see Survival Guide (p177)

Currency
Pound sterling (£)

Language
English

Visas
Generally not needed for stays of up to six months. The UK is no longer a member of the EU.

Money
ATMs widespread. Major credit cards accepted everywhere.

Mobile Phones
Uses the GSM 900/1800 network. Local SIM cards can be used in European and Australian phones.

Time
Edinburgh is on GMT; during British Summer Time (BST; last Sunday in March to last Saturday in October) clocks are one hour ahead of GMT.

Tipping
Tip restaurant waiting staff 10% to 15% unless service is included.

Daily Budget

Budget: Less than £50
Dorm bed: £15–30
Lunch special or food shopping at market: £5–10
Many museums and galleries: free

Midrange: £50–150
Double room: £80–100
Two-course dinner with glass of wine: £40
Live music in pub: free–£10

Top End: More than £150
Double room in boutique/four-star hotel: £175–300
Three-course dinner (including wine) in top restaurant: £70–120
Taxi across town: £15

Advance Planning

Six months before Book accommodation for the August festival period. Book a table at the Witchery by the Castle restaurant. (p66)

Two months before Book hotel or B&B accommodation; reserve tables in top restaurants; book car hire.

One month before Buy tickets online for Edinburgh Castle (p42); check listings for theatre, live music etc and book tickets.

Arriving in Edinburgh

Most visitors arrive at Edinburgh Airport (www.edinburghairport.com), 8 miles west of the city centre, or at Edinburgh Waverley train station, right in the heart of the city between the Old Town and New Town.

✈ Edinburgh Airport

Airlink 100 bus runs from the airport to South St David St every 12 minutes from 4am to 1am and every 30 minutes through the night. Trams run from the airport to the city centre (33 minutes, every six to eight minutes from 6.15am to 10.45pm). An airport taxi to the city centre takes about 30 minutes.

🚇 Waverley Train Station

Taxi rank in station. Short walk to Princes St, where trams and buses depart to all areas of the city.

Getting Around

🚌 Bus

Best way of getting from the suburbs to the centre, and for north–south trips. Despite dedicated bus lanes, buses can get held up during rush hours.

🚊 Tram

Fast and frequent service from the airport to York Place in the east of the city centre, via Murrayfield Stadium, Haymarket, the West End and Princes St.

🚕 Taxi

Great for late-night journeys, but fares can be expensive unless there are four people sharing.

🚲 Bike

Hire a bike and escape to the countryside via the Water of Leith Walkway, or the Union Canal towpath.

MAX BLINKHORN/GETTY IMAGES ©

Edinburgh Neighbourhoods

Stockbridge (p133)
A former village with its own distinct identity, stylish and quirky shops and a good choice of pubs and restaurants.

New Town (p91)
Georgian terraces lined with designer boutiques, wine bars and cocktail lounges, plus Princes Street Gardens and the perfect viewpoint of Calton Hill.

West End & Dean Village (p119)
More Georgian elegance and upmarket shops, leading down to the picturesque Dean Village in the wooded valley of Water of Leith.

South Edinburgh (p161)
A peaceful residential area of Victorian tenement flats and spacious garden villas; not much in the way of tourist attractions, but good walking territory and many good restaurants and pubs.

Royal Botanic Garden

Scottish National Portrait Gallery

Scottish National Gallery of Modern Art

Real Mary King's Close

Princes Street Gardens

Edinburgh Castle

Leith (p147)

Redeveloped industrial docklands now occupied by restaurants, bars and the huge Ocean Terminal shopping mall, home to the Royal Yacht Britannia.

Holyrood & Arthur's Seat (p77)

At the foot of the Royal Mile, contains the Scottish Parliament and the Palace of Holyroodhouse, and is the gateway to the craggy parkland of Arthur's Seat.

Royal Yacht Britannia

Scottish Parliament Building

Palace of Holyroodhouse

National Museum of Scotland

Old Town (p41)

A maze of narrow wynds (alleys) and cobbled streets, strung out along the Royal Mile, home to the city's main historical sights, including Edinburgh Castle.

Explore
Edinburgh

Old Town **41**

Holyrood & Arthur's Seat **77**

New Town **91**

West End & Dean Village **119**

Stockbridge **133**

Leith **147**

South Edinburgh **161**

Worth a Trip 👀

Rosslyn Chapel 174

Edinburgh's Walking Tours 🚶

Explore the Old Town's Hidden History 52

From Castle to Palace 54

A Walk Through Holyrood Park 82

Charlotte Square to Calton Hill 96

Hit the Shops in New Town 98

A Sunday Stroll Around Stockbridge 136

Busker outside Edinburgh Castle (p42) WILL SALTER/LONELY PLANET ©

Explore ⊛
Old Town

Edinburgh's Old Town is a maze of historic masonry riddled with closes, stairs and wynds leading off the cobbled ravine of the Royal Mile, linking Edinburgh Castle to the Palace of Holyroodhouse. The Old Town tenements support a dwindling city-centre community – many flats have been converted to short-term holiday lets – with the street level crammed with cafes, restaurants, bars, hostels and souvenir shops.

The Short List

○ **Edinburgh Castle (p42)** *Visiting Scotland's most popular attraction, a craggy cluster of museums, militaria and the Scottish crown jewels.*

○ **Real Mary King's Close (p46)** *Taking an atmospheric guided tour of this buried medieval street, sealed off in the 18th century.*

○ **National Museum of Scotland (p48)** *Charting the history of Scotland from its geological beginnings to the present day.*

○ **Royal Mile wynds (p54)** *Leaving the crowds behind among the Old Town's maze of hidden alleyways.*

○ **Greyfriars Kirkyard (p60)** *Scaring yourself silly on a ghost tour of Edinburgh's most haunted cemetery.*

Getting There & Around

🚌 Service 35 runs along the lower part of the Royal Mile from South Bridge to the Scottish Parliament Building and the Palace of Holyroodhouse. Buses 23, 27, 41 and 42 run along the Mound and George IV Bridge, crossing the Royal Mile near St Giles Cathedral.

Neighbourhood Map on p56

West Bow WESTEND61/GETTY IMAGES ©

Top Sight 📷
Edinburgh Castle

The brooding black crags of Castle Rock, rising above the western end of Princes St, are the very reason for Edinburgh's existence. This rocky hill was the most easily defended hilltop on the invasion route between England and central Scotland. Today it is one of Scotland's most atmospheric and popular tourist attractions.

◉ MAP P56, A4

www.edinburghcastle.scot

Castle Esplanade

adult/child £17.50/10.50, audio guide £3.50/1.50

🕘 9.30am-6pm Apr-Sep, to 5pm Oct-Mar, last entry 1hr before closing

🚌 23, 27, 41, 42

The Esplanade

The castle's **Esplanade** is a parade ground dating from 1820, with superb views south over the city towards the Pentland Hills. At its western end is the **Entrance Gateway**, dating from 1888 and flanked by statues of Robert the Bruce and William Wallace. Above the gate is the Royal Standard of Scotland – a red lion rampant on a gold field – and the Scottish royal motto in Latin, 'Nemo me impune lacessit'. This translates into Scots as 'wha daur meddle wi' me', and into English as 'watch it, pal' (OK, it literally means 'no one provokes me with impunity').

One O'Clock Gun

Inside the entrance a cobbled lane leads up beneath the 16th-century **Portcullis Gate**, topped by the 19th-century **Argyle Tower**, and past the cannon of the Argyle and Mills Mount Batteries. The battlements here have great views over the New Town to the Firth of Forth. At the far end of Mills Mount Battery is the **One O'Clock Gun**, a gleaming WWII 25-pounder that fires an ear-splitting time signal at 1pm every day (except Sunday, Christmas Day and Good Friday).

St Margaret's Chapel

South of Mills Mount the road curls up leftward through **Foog's Gate** to the highest part of Castle Rock, crowned by the tiny **St Margaret's Chapel**, the oldest surviving building in Edinburgh. It's a simple Romanesque structure that was probably built by David I or Alexander I in memory of their mother, Queen Margaret, sometime around 1130 (she was canonised in 1250). Following Cromwell's capture of the castle in 1650 it was used to store ammunition until it was restored at the order of Queen Victoria; it was rededicated in 1934. The tiny stained-glass windows – depicting Margaret, St Andrew, St Columba, St Ninian and William Wallace – date from the 1920s.

★ Top Tips

o Avoid ticket-office queues by purchasing your tickets online via the Edinburgh Castle website.

o It's worth hiring an audio guide (£3.50) to provide extra context for the various historical attractions you'll see.

o Time your visit to coincide with the firing of the One O'Clock Gun.

✕ Take a Break

o The **Redcoat Café** (www.edinburghcastle. scot/see-and-do/ eat; Crown Sq; mains £5-10; ⏰9.30am-5pm Apr-Oct, 10am-4pm Nov-Mar; ♿; ☐23, 27, 41, 42) serves good lunches.

o Just a few yards downhill from the castle on the Royal Mile, Cannonball Restaurant (p63) has top-quality Scottish cuisine.

Mons Meg

Immediately north of St Margaret's Chapel is **Mons Meg**, a giant 15th-century siege gun built at Mons in Belgium in 1449. The gun was last fired in 1681, as a birthday salute for the future James VII/II, when its barrel burst. Take a peek over the wall to the north of the chapel and you'll see a charming little garden that was used as a **pet cemetery** for officers' dogs.

Great Hall

The main group of buildings on the summit of Castle Rock are ranged around Crown Sq, dominated by the shrine of the **Scottish National War Memorial**. Opposite is the **Great Hall**, built for James IV (r 1488–1513) as a ceremonial hall and used as a meeting place for the Scottish Parliament until 1639. Its most remarkable feature is the original 16th-century hammer-beam roof.

Prisons of War Exhibition

The **Castle Vaults** beneath the Great Hall (entered on the west side of Crown Sq) were used variously as storerooms, bakeries and prisons. The vaults have been restored to how they were in the 18th and early 19th centuries, when they were used as a prison for soldiers captured during the American War of Independence and the Napoleonic Wars. Original graffiti carved by French and American prisoners can be seen on the ancient wooden doors.

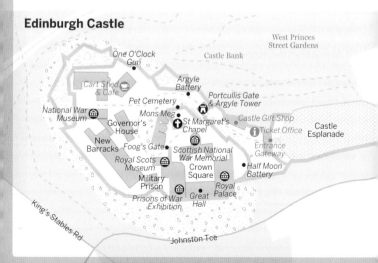

Edinburgh Castle

West Princes Street Gardens
Castle Bank
One O'Clock Gun
Cart Shed & Cafe
Argyle Battery
Portcullis Gate & Argyle Tower
Pet Cemetery
National War Museum
Mons Meg
St Margaret's Chapel
Castle Gift Shop
Governor's House
Ticket Office
Castle Esplanade
New Barracks
Foog's Gate
Scottish National War Memorial
Entrance Gateway
Royal Scots Museum
Crown Square
Half Moon Battery
Military Prison
Royal Palace
Prisons of War Exhibition
Great Hall
King's Stables Rd
Johnston Tce

The Stone of Destiny

On St Andrew's Day 1996, with much pomp and circumstance, a block of sandstone 26.5 inches by 16.5 inches by 11 inches in size (67cm by 42cm by 28cm), with rusted iron hoops at either end, was installed in Edinburgh Castle. For the previous 700 years it had lain beneath the Coronation Chair in London's Westminster Abbey, where almost every English – and later British – monarch from Edward II in 1308 to Elizabeth II in 1953 had sat during their coronation ceremonies.

This is the legendary Stone of Destiny, on which Scottish kings placed their feet (not their bums; the English got that bit wrong) during their coronation. It was stolen from Scone Abbey near Perth by Edward I of England in 1296 and taken to London, where it remained for seven centuries, an enduring symbol of Scotland's subjugation by England.

It returned to the political limelight in 1996, when the Westminster government arranged for its return in an attempt to boost the flagging popularity of the Conservative Party in Scotland prior to a general election. (The stunt failed: Scotland returned no Conservative MPs at the ensuing election.)

Honours of Scotland

The **Royal Palace**, built during the 15th and 16th centuries, houses a series of historical tableaux leading to the highlight of the castle: a strongroom housing the **Honours of Scotland** (the Scottish crown jewels), among the oldest surviving crown jewels in Europe. Locked away in a chest following the *Act of Union* in 1707, the crown (made in 1540 from the gold of Robert the Bruce's 14th-century coronet), sword and sceptre lay forgotten until they were unearthed at the instigation of novelist Sir Walter Scott in 1818. Also on display here is the Stone of Destiny.

Among the neighbouring **Royal Apartments** is the bedchamber where Mary, Queen of Scots, gave birth to her son James VI, who was to unite the crowns of Scotland and England in 1603.

Top Sight 📷

Real Mary King's Close

Edinburgh's 18th-century city chambers were built over the sealed-off remains of Mary King's Close, and the lower levels of this medieval Old Town alley have survived almost unchanged amid the foundations for 250 years. Now open to the public, this spooky, subterranean labyrinth gives a fascinating insight into the everyday life of 17th-century Edinburgh.

◉ MAP P56, D3

📞 0131-225 0672

www.realmarykings
close.com

2 Warriston's Close

adult/child £17.95/11.25

🕑 hours vary

🚌 23, 27, 41, 42

The Tenement Room

A drama student in period costume will take you on a guided tour through the vaults while practising his or her dramatic enunciation and corny jokes. The scripted tour, complete with ghostly tales and gruesome tableaux, can seem a little naff, milking the scary and scatological aspects of the close's history for all they're worth. But there are things of genuine interest to see: there's something about the crumbling 17th-century **tenement room** that makes the hair rise on the back of your neck, with tufts of horsehair poking from collapsing lath-and-plaster walls that bear the ghost of a pattern, and the ancient smell of stone and dust thick in your nostrils.

Wee Annie's Room

In one of the former bedrooms off the close, a psychic once claimed to have been approached by the ghost of a little girl called Annie. It's hard to tell what's more frightening – the story of the ghostly child, or the bizarre heap of tiny dolls and teddies left in a corner by sympathetic visitors.

The Foot of the Close

Perhaps the most atmospheric part of the tour is at the end, when you stand at the foot of Mary King's Close itself. You are effectively standing in a buried street, with the old tenement walls rising on either side, and the weight of the 11 storeys of the city chambers above – and some 250 years of history – pressing down all around you.

★ Top Tips

o Tours are limited to 20 people at a time, so book online at least 24 hours in advance to secure a place.

o The tour includes a lot of stairs and uneven stone surfaces – wear suitable shoes.

o There are lots of enclosed spaces – not recommended if you suffer from claustrophobia!

o Children under the age of five are not admitted.

✗ Take a Break

o Enjoy pizza at a pavement table at **Gordon's Trattoria** (☑0131-225 7992; www.gordonstrattoria.com; 231 High St; mains £12-20; ⊙noon-11pm Sun-Thu, to midnight Fri & Sat; ⍟; ⍟all South Bridge buses), a short distance downhill.

o For a more sophisticated seafood lunch, head to Ondine (p63), uphill and round the corner.

Top Sight

National Museum of Scotland

The golden stone and striking modern architecture of the National Museum's new building (1998) make it one of the city's most distinctive landmarks. The modern building's five floors trace the history of Scotland from geological beginnings to the present, and connect with the original Victorian museum, which covers natural history, world cultures, archaeology, design and fashion, and science and technology.

◉ MAP P56, E5

☏ 0300 123 6789

www.nms.ac.uk/national-museum-of-scotland

Chambers St, EH1 1JF

admission free

🕙 10am-5pm

🚹

🚌 35, 45

TAKASHI IMAGES/SHUTTERSTOCK ©

Grand Gallery

The museum's main entrance, in the middle of Chambers St, leads into an atmospheric entrance hall occupying what used to be the museum cellars. Stairs lead up into the light of the Victorian **Grand Gallery**, a spectacular glass-roofed atrium lined with cast-iron pillars and balconies; this was the centrepiece of the original Victorian museum. It was designed in the 1860s by Captain Francis Fowke of the Royal Engineers, who also created the Royal Albert Hall in London, and parts of London's Victoria and Albert Museum.

Crowds gather on the hour to watch the chiming of the **Millennium Clock Tower**. Built in 1999 to commemorate the best and worst of human history, and inspired by mechanical marvels such as Prague's Astronomical Clock, it is more a kinetic sculpture than a clock, crammed with amusing and thought-provoking symbols and animated figures.

Animal World

A door at the eastern end of the Grand Gallery leads into **Animal World**, one of the most impressive of the old building's exhibits. No dusty, static regiments of stuffed creatures here, but a beautiful and dynamic display of animals apparently caught in the act of leaping, flying or swimming, arranged in groups that illustrate different means of locomotion, methods of feeding and modes of reproduction. Extinct creatures, including a full-size skeleton of a Tyrannosaurus rex, mingle with the extant.

Window on the World

The exhibits ranged around the balconies of the Grand Gallery are billed as a **'Window on the World'**, showcasing more than 800 items from the museum's collections, ranging from the **world's largest scrimshaw carving**, occupying

★ Top Tips

o Begin at the main entrance in the middle of Chambers St, rather than the modern tower at the western end of the street. You'll find an info desk, a cloak-room, toilets and a cafe-restaurant.

o Free, one-hour guided tours depart at 11am, 1pm and 3pm, each covering a different theme.

o You can download PDFs of museum trails for children to follow – check out the Family Puzzle Trail.

✕ Take a Break

o The **Museum Brasserie** (☏0131-225 4040; www.benugo.com/restaurants/museum-brasserie; Chambers St; mains £7-14; ⊙9am-5pm; ♿; ☒35, 45) in the basement of the Victorian part of the museum serves light lunches.

o The **Balcony Café** (Level 3) is open daily from 10.30am to 4.30pm for tea, coffee, home baking, soup, sandwiches, salads and children's lunch boxes.

two full-size sperm-whale jawbones, to a four-seat racing bicycle dating from 1898.

Hawthornden Court

A suite of science and technology galleries link the Grand Gallery of the old museum to **Hawthornden Court** in the new building, with exhibits that include Dolly the sheep, the first mammal ever to be cloned, historic aircraft, and a section of a particle accelerator from CERN.

Early People Gallery

Stairs at the far end of Hawthornden Court lead down to the **Early People Gallery** on Level 0, decorated with intriguing humanoid sculptures by Sir Eduardo Paolozzi and beautiful installations by sculptor Andy Golds-

worthy, including huge stacks of old roofing slates, cleverly arranged scrap timber and a sphere made entirely of whale bones. Look out for the **Cramond Lioness**, a Roman funerary sculpture of a lion gripping a human head in her jaws (it was discovered in the River Almond, on the western edge of Edinburgh, in 1997), and the 22kg of Roman silver that makes up the **Traprain Treasure**. It was buried in the 5th century CE and discovered in 1919, and is the biggest known hoard of Roman silver ever to be found.

Kingdom of the Scots

From the Early People Gallery you work your way upwards through the history of Scotland. Highlights of the medieval **Kingdom of the Scots** galleries, on Levels 1 and 2, include

Roof terrace

the **Monymusk Reliquary**, a tiny silver casket dating from 750 CE, which is said to have been carried into battle with Robert the Bruce at Bannockburn in 1314; and the famous **Lewis chessmen**, charming 12th-century chess pieces carved from walrus ivory, that were discovered on Uig beach on the Isle of Lewis.

Death Comes In...

The Daith Comes In (Death Comes In) exhibit on Level 4 is a goth's paradise of wooden hearses, jet jewellery, and mourning bracelets made from human hair, as well as the 'mortsafes' that once protected newly buried corpses from the ravages of the body snatchers (p61). But the most fascinating objects on display here are the mysterious **Arthur's Seat coffins**. Discovered in a cave in 1836 by some boys hunting rabbits, these miniature coffins (only eight of the original 17 survive) are less than 10cm long and have tiny wooden figures inside. They may have been part of a mock burial for the victims of Edinburgh's most famous body snatchers, Burke and Hare, who sold their murdered victims to the city's anatomy professor.

Leaving Scotland

Level 6 of the museum is given over to the 20th century, with galleries devoted to war, industry and daily life illustrated by personal stories, film clips and iconic objects such as a **set of bagpipes** that was played at the Battle of the Somme in 1916. There is also an exhibition called **Leaving Scotland**, containing stories of the Scottish diaspora that emigrated to begin new lives in Canada, Australia, the USA and other places, from the 18th century right up until the 1960s.

Roof Terrace

Before you leave, find the elevator in the corner of Level 6, near the war gallery, and go up to the roof terrace to enjoy a fantastic view across the city to the castle ramparts.

Walking Tour 🥾

Explore the Old Town's Hidden History

Edinburgh's Old Town extends to the south of the Royal Mile, descending into the valley of the Grassmarket and Cowgate, which is crossed by the arches of George IV Bridge and South Bridge. This difference in levels has created a maze of narrow closes, wynds and staircases, which lend an adventurous air to exploring its many hidden corners.

Walk Facts

Start Victoria Terrace; bus: Victoria St

Finish South Bridge Vaults; bus: South Bridge

Length 1.5 miles; one hour

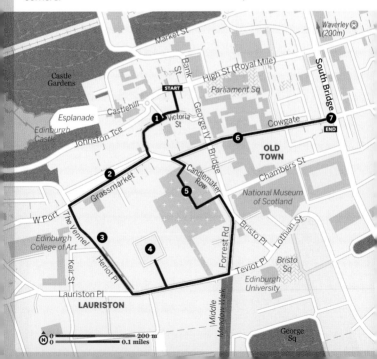

❶ Victoria Terrace

From the Lawnmarket at the top of the Royal Mile, dive down Fisher's Close, which leads you onto the delightful Victoria Terrace. Wander along to the right, enjoying the view – Maxie's Bistro (p68) is a great place to stop for lunch or a drink.

❷ Grassmarket

Descend the stairs in the middle of the terrace and continue downhill to the Grassmarket. The site of a cattle market from the 15th century until the start of the 20th, the Grassmarket was also the city's place of execution, and martyred Covenanters are commemorated by a monument at the eastern end.

❸ Flodden Wall

Turn left up the flight of stairs known as the Vennel. At the top of the steps on the left is the Flodden Wall, one of the few surviving fragments of the city wall built in the 16th century as protection against a feared English invasion. Beyond it stretches the Telfer Wall extension.

❹ George Heriot's School

Turn left along Lauriston Pl to find George Heriot's School, among the most impressive Old Town buildings. Built in the 17th century with funds bequeathed by George Heriot (banker to King James VI), it was originally a school for orphans, but became a fee-paying school in 1886. It's open to the public on **Doors Open Day** (www.doorsopendays.org.uk) in September.

❺ Greyfriar's Kirkyard

Hemmed in by high walls and overlooked by the castle, Greyfriars Kirkyard is one of Edinburgh's most evocative spots, a peaceful green oasis dotted with elaborate monuments. Many famous Edinburgh names are buried here.

❻ Cowgate

The Cowgate – the long, dark ravine leading eastward from the Grassmarket – was once the road along which cattle were driven from the pastures around Arthur's Seat to the safety of the city walls, or to be sold at market. To the right are the new law courts, followed by Tailors Hall, now a hotel and bar but formerly the meeting place of the 'Companie of Tailzeours' (Tailors' Guild).

❼ South Bridge Vaults

South Bridge passes over the Cowgate in a single arch, but there are another nine arches hidden on either side, surrounded by later buildings. The ones to the north can be visited on a guided tour with Mercat Tours (p66); those to the south are occupied by a nightclub, the Caves (p71).

Walking Tour 🚶

From Castle to Palace

Edinburgh Castle, the Palace of Holyroodhouse and the Scottish Parliament are what make Edinburgh Scotland's capital. This walk links the city's most iconic sights by following (mostly) the Royal Mile, the ancient processional route followed by kings and queens travelling between castle and palace. Our route occasionally shifts sideways to explore the narrow closes and wynds that lend the Old Town its unique, historic atmosphere.

Walk Facts

Start Edinburgh Castle; bus: Victoria St

Finish Palace of Holyroodhouse; bus: Scottish Parliament

Length 1.5 miles; one hour

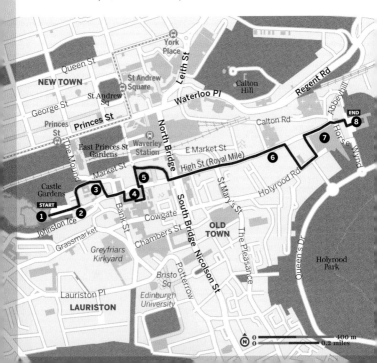

❶ Edinburgh Castle

Dominating the city from its superb defensive position, Edinburgh Castle (p42) is one of Britain's most impressive fortresses. Check out the Scottish crown jewels, wander through the former prisons in the Castle Vaults, and try not to jump when the One O'Clock Gun is fired.

❷ Scotch Whisky Experience

After enjoying the views from the **Castle Esplanade**, head down the Royal Mile. On the left you'll pass the **Witches Well** (a fountain commemorating those executed on suspicion of witchcraft) before reaching the Scotch Whisky Experience (p58).

❸ Writers' Museum

Descend Ramsay Lane to the twin towers of Edinburgh's **New College**, and see the **statue of John Knox** in the courtyard. Return to the Royal Mile via **Lady Stair's Close**, a picturesque Old Town alley, and the Writers' Museum (p59).

❹ St Giles Cathedral

Continue down the High St to St Giles Cathedral (p58), Edinburgh's most important church. Follow Parliament Sq around the south side of the church, and take a look at Parliament Hall (p63) and the **Mercat Cross**.

❺ Real Mary King's Close

Back on the High St is the Georgian facade of the **city chambers** (seat of Edinburgh city council), which was built over a medieval Old Town alley with eerie remains you can explore on a tour of the Real Mary King's Close (p46).

❻ Museum of Edinburgh

Descend **Advocate's Close**, one of the most atmospheric of the Old Town's wynds, then climb back to the Royal Mile along **Cockburn St**, lined with trendy boutiques. Continue down the High St, past John Knox House (p60), to the Museum of Edinburgh (p58).

❼ Scottish Parliament Building

Opposite **Canongate Kirk**, go down Crighton's Close past the **Scottish Poetry Library**, then left and left again up Reid's Close, to see the Scottish Parliament Building (p80).

❽ Palace of Holyroodhouse

The Royal Mile ends at the ornate gates of the Palace of Holyroodhouse (p78), the official residence of the royal family when they're in town.

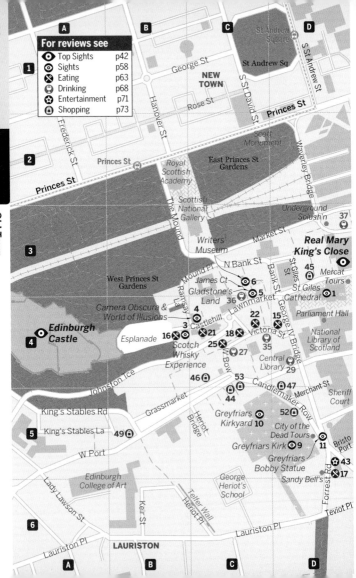

For reviews see

- Top Sights   p42
- Sights   p58
- Eating   p63
- Drinking   p68
- Entertainment   p71
- Shopping   p73

NEW TOWN

George St

St Andrew Sq

St Andrew Square

Hanover St

Rose St

Frederick St

Princes St

Scott Monument

Princes St

Royal Scottish Academy

East Princes St Gardens

Princes St

Waverley Bridge

The Mound

Scottish National Gallery

Writers' Museum

Underground Soush'n 37

Market St

Real Mary King's Close

N Bank St

West Princes St Gardens

Mound Pl

James Ct 6

Gladstone's Land 5

Bank St

St Giles St

Mercat Tours 45

St Giles Cathedral 1

Lawnmarket

36

Parliament Hall

Camera Obscura & World of Illusions

Ramsay Ln

Castlehill 4 3

22

George IV Bridge

15

National Library of Scotland

Edinburgh Castle

Esplanade 16

21 18

Victoria St

25 27

W Bow

35

Central Library 29

Johnston Tce

46

53

Candlemaker Row

47

Merchant St

Sheriff Court

44

Scotch Whisky Experience

Grassmarket

King's Stables Rd

Heriot Bridge

Greyfriars Kirkyard 10

52

City of the Dead Tours

King's Stables La

49

W Port

Greyfriars Kirk 9

11

Bristo Port

Edinburgh College of Art

Lady Lawson St

Keir St

Telfer Wall

Heriot Pl

George Heriot's School

Greyfriars Bobby Statue

Sandy Bell's

Forrest Rd

43

17

Lauriston Pl

LAURISTON

Lauriston Pl

Teviot Pl

Lauriston Pl

E   F   G   Calton Hill   H

Leith St

Waterloo Pl

St Andrew's House

Royal High School

1

Regent Rd

Calton Rd

Calton Rd

Canongate Kirkyard

◉ **12**

2

Waverley Station

North Bridge

New St

Sibbald Walk

People's Story

◉ **8**

◉ **2**

Fruitmarket Gallery

City Art Centre

E Market St

Market St

Jeffrey St

Scotsman Steps

Cookie

Pie in the Sky

Cockburn St

Museum Context

Edinburgh Tourist Office

High St (Royal Mile)

Old Fishmarket Cl

✕ **24**

Tron Sq

28 ⊙

Cowgate

⊙ **30**

Guthrie St

Chambers St

W College St

National Museum of Scotland

32 33
⊙   ⊙

Bristo Pl

Lothian St

Bristo Sq

Edinburgh University

Marshall St

◉ **14**

John Knox House

20

Cranston St

Canongate (Royal Mile)

Museum of Edinburgh

50 ⊙ ◉ **7**

✕ **19**

48

St Mary's St

54

✕ **26**

Blackfriars St

S Gray's Cl

42
★

Niddry St

Blair St

41
★

38
★

40   **39**
★   ★

Infirmary St

51 ⊙

South Bridge

S College St

Edinburgh University

Edinburgh Festival Theatre

Potterrow

✕ **31**

13
◉

Dovecot Studios

Drummond St

Edinburgh University Campus

Surgeons' Hall Museums

Hill Pl

Nicolson Sq

Nicolson St

23
✕

⊙ **34**

Holyrood Rd

St John's Hill

St John St

3

Pleasance Sports Centre

4

Roxburgh Pl

E Adam St

The Pleasance

Viewcraig Gdns

5

W Richmond St

Brown St

Davie St

Holyrood Park

6

⬙ 0   200 m
0   0.1 miles

E   F   G   H

OLD TOWN

Sights

St Giles Cathedral
CHURCH

1 ⊙ MAP P56, D3

The great grey bulk of St Giles Cathedral dates largely from the 15th century, but much of it was restored in the 19th century. One of the most interesting corners of the kirk is the **Thistle Chapel**, built in 1911 for the Knights of the Most Ancient & Most Noble Order of the Thistle. The elaborately carved Gothic-style stalls have canopies topped with the helms and arms of the 16 knights – look out for the bagpipe-playing angel amid the vaulting. (www.stgilescathedral.org. uk; High St; admission free; ⏰9am-7pm Mon-Fri, to 5pm Sat, 1-5pm Sun Apr-Oct, 9am-5pm Mon-Sat, 1-5pm Sun Nov-Mar; 🚌23, 27, 41, 42)

Museum of Edinburgh
MUSEUM

2 ⊙ MAP P56, H2

You can't miss the colourful facade of Huntly House (it featured in Season 3 of the TV series *Outlander*), opposite the Tolbooth clock on the Royal Mile. Built in 1570, it houses a museum covering Edinburgh from prehistory to the present. Exhibits of national importance include an original copy of the National Covenant of 1638, but the big crowd-pleaser is the dog collar and feeding bowl that once belonged to Greyfriars Bobby (p61), the city's most famous canine citizen. (📞0131-529 4143; www.edinburgh museums.org.uk; 142 Canongate; admission free; ⏰10am-5pm Mon & Thu-Sat, noon-5pm Sun; 🚌300)

Scotch Whisky Experience
MUSEUM

3 ⊙ MAP P56, B4

A former school houses this multimedia centre that takes you through the making of whisky, from barley to bottle, in a series of exhibits, demonstrations and talks that combine sight, sound and smell, including the world's largest collection of malt whiskies (3384 bottles!). The pricier tours include extensive whisky tastings and samples of Scottish cuisine. There's also a restaurant (p67) that serves traditional Scottish dishes with, where possible, a dash of whisky thrown in. (www. scotchwhiskyexperience.co.uk; 354 Castlehill; adult/child from £17/8; ⏰10am-6pm Apr-Jul, to 5pm Aug-Mar; 🚌23, 27, 41, 42)

Camera Obscura & World of Illusions
MUSEUM

4 ⊙ MAP P56, C4

Edinburgh's camera obscura is a curious 19th-century device – in constant use since 1853 – that uses lenses and mirrors to throw a live image of the city onto a large horizontal screen. The accompanying commentary is entertaining and the whole experience has a quirky charm, complemented by an intriguing exhibition dedicated to illusions of all kinds. Stairs lead up through various displays to the

Outlook Tower, which offers great views over the city. (www.camera-obscura.co.uk; Castlehill; adult/child £16.50/12.50; ☺9am-10pm Jul & Aug, 9.30am-8pm Apr-Jun, Sep & Oct, 9.30am-7pm Nov-Mar; ☐23, 27, 41, 42)

Gladstone's Land

HISTORIC BUILDING

5 MAP P56, C3

One of Edinburgh's most prominent 17th-century merchants was Thomas Gledstanes, who in 1617 purchased the tenement later known as Gladstone's Land. It contains fine painted ceilings, walls and beams, and some splendid furniture from the 17th and 18th centuries. The building has undergone a major refurbishment, scheduled to reopen by summer

2021 with a traditional ice-cream parlour on street level, exhibitions on the middle floors, and holiday apartments on the upper floors. (NTS; ☎0131-226 5856; www.nts.org.uk; 477 Lawnmarket; ☐23, 27, 41, 42)

Writers' Museum

MUSEUM

6 MAP P56, C3

Tucked down a close between the Royal Mile and the Mound you'll find Lady Stair's House (1622), home to this museum that contains manuscripts and memorabilia belonging to three of Scotland's most famous writers: Robert Burns, Sir Walter Scott and Robert Louis Stevenson. (☎0131-529 4901; www.edinburghmuseums.org.uk; Lady Stair's Close; admission free; ☺10am-5pm; ☐23, 27, 41, 42)

Old Town Sights

St Giles Cathedral

CHRISTIAN MUELLER/SHUTTERSTOCK ©

Ghost Tours

The **City of the Dead Tours** (Map p56; D5; 📞0131-225 9044; www.cityofthedeadtours.com; 26a Candlemaker; adult/concession £14/10; ⏰9pm Easter-Oct, 8.30pm Tue & Thu-Sat Nov-Easter) of Greyfriars Kirkyard are probably the scariest of Edinburgh's ghost tours. Many people have reported encounters with the McKenzie Poltergeist, the ghost of a 17th-century judge who persecuted the Covenanters (supporters of the Scottish Presbyterian church, in defiance of King Charles I's attempts to impose Roman Catholicism) and who now haunts their former prison in a corner of the kirkyard. Not suitable for young children!

John Knox House
HISTORIC BUILDING

7 📍 MAP P56, F3

The Royal Mile narrows at the foot of High St, beside the jutting facade of John Knox House. This is the oldest surviving tenement in Edinburgh, dating from around 1490. John Knox, an influential church reformer and leader of the Protestant Reformation in Scotland, is thought to have lived here from 1561 to 1572. The labyrinthine interior has some beautiful painted-timber ceilings and an interesting display on Knox's life and

work. (www.scottishstorytellingcentre.com/john-knox-house; 43-45 High St; adult/child £6/1; ⏰10am-6pm daily Jul & Aug, Mon-Sat Sep-Jun; 🚌35)

People's Story
MUSEUM

8 📍 MAP P56, H2

One of the surviving symbols of the Canongate district's former independence is the **Canongate Tolbooth**. Built in 1591, it served successively as a collection point for tolls (taxes), a council house, a courtroom and a jail. With picturesque turrets and a projecting clock, it's an interesting example of 16th-century architecture. It now houses a fascinating museum called the People's Story, which covers the life, work and pastimes of ordinary Edinburgh folk from the 18th century to today. (www.edinburghmuseums.org.uk; 163 Canongate; admission free; ⏰10am-5pm Wed-Sat, noon-5pm Sun; 🚌35)

Greyfriars Kirk
CHURCH

9 📍 MAP P56, D5

One of Edinburgh's most famous churches, Greyfriars Kirk was built on the site of a Franciscan friary and opened for worship on Christmas Day 1620. (www.greyfriarskirk.com; Greyfriars Pl; ⏰10.30am-4.30pm Mon-Fri, 11am-2pm Sat Apr-Oct, 11am-3pm Thu Nov-Mar; 🚌2, 23, 27, 35, 41, 42, 45)

Greyfriars Kirkyard
CEMETERY

10 📍 MAP P56, C5

Greyfriars Kirkyard is one of Edinburgh's most evocative cemeteries, a peaceful green oasis dotted with elaborate monuments. Many famous Edinburgh names are buried here, including poet Allan Ramsay (1686–1758); architect William Adam (1689–1748); and William Smellie (1740–95), editor of the first edition of the *Encyclopaedia Britannica*. If you want to experience the graveyard at its scariest – inside a burial vault, in the dark, at night – go on a City of the Dead guided tour. (www.greyfriar skirk.com; Candlemaker Row; ☉24hr; 🚌2, 23, 27, 35, 41, 42, 45)

Greyfriars Bobby Statue
MONUMENT

11 ◉ MAP P56, D5

Probably the most popular photo opportunity in Edinburgh, the

life-size statue of Greyfriars Bobby, a Skye terrier who captured the hearts of the British public in the late 19th century, stands outside Greyfriars Kirkyard. From 1858 to 1872 the wee dog maintained a vigil over the grave of his master, an Edinburgh police officer. The story was immortalised in a novel by Eleanor Atkinson in 1912, and in 1961 was made into a movie by – who else? – Walt Disney. (cnr George IV Bridge & Candlemaker Row; 🚌2, 23, 27, 35, 41, 42, 45)

Canongate Kirkyard
CHURCH

12 ◉ MAP P56, H2

The attractive curved gable of the Canongate Kirk, built in 1688, overlooks a kirkyard that contains the graves of several famous

The Resurrection Men

Edinburgh has long had a reputation for being at the cutting edge of medical research. In the early 19th century this led to a shortage of cadavers with which the city's anatomists could satisfy their curiosity, and an illegal trade in dead bodies emerged.

The readiest supply of corpses was to be found in the city's graveyards. Grave robbers – known as 'resurrection men' – plundered newly buried coffins and sold the cadavers to the anatomists, who turned a blind eye to the source of their research material.

William Burke and William Hare took the body-snatching business a step further, deciding to create their own supply of fresh cadavers by resorting to murder. Between December 1827 and October 1828 they killed at least 16 people, selling their bodies to the surgeon Robert Knox.

When the law finally caught up with them, Hare testified against Burke, who was hanged outside St Giles Cathedral in January 1829. In an ironic twist, his body was given to the anatomy school for public dissection.

people, including economist Adam Smith, author of *The Wealth of Nations*; Agnes Maclehose (the 'Clarinda' of Robert Burns' love poems); and poet Robert Fergusson (1750–74; there's a statue of him on the street outside the church). An information board just inside the gate lists notable graves and their locations. (www.canongatekirk.org.uk/kirkyard; Canongate; ☾dawn-dusk; ☐35)

Dovecot Studios ARTS CENTRE

13 ◉ MAP P56, F4

A world-class tapestry studio and contemporary arts-and-crafts centre housed in what was once Edinburgh's oldest public baths, Dovecot has a remarkable history dating back a century. You can watch the weavers at work from a viewing platform above the workshop. The shop and the cafe, which is run by Leo's Beanery, are excellent, too. (☎0131-550 3660; www.dovecotstudios.com; 10 Infirmary St; admission free; ☾10am-5pm Mon-Sat; ☐all South Bridge buses)

City Art Centre GALLERY

14 ◉ MAP P56, E3

This art centre comprises six floors of exhibitions with a variety of themes, including an extensive collection of Scottish art. Fees apply for special exhibitions. (www.edinburghmuseums.org.uk; 2 Market St; admission free; ☾10am-5pm Tue-Sun; ☖; ☐3, 5, 8, 29, 45)

City Art Centre

AIVITA ARIKA/SHUTTERSTOCK ©

Parliament Hall

Before you visit the Scottish Parliament Building, take a look at the magnificent 17th-century **Parliament Hall** (Map p56, D4; ☑0131-348 5355; 11 Parliament Sq; admission free; ☉10am-4pm Mon-Fri; ☐2, 23, 27, 41). Tucked behind St Giles Cathedral, it has an original oak hammer-beam roof, and is where the original Scottish Parliament met before its dissolution in 1707. Now used by lawyers and their clients as a meeting place, it's open to the public. As you enter from Parliament Sq (there's a sign outside saying 'Parliament Hall; Court of Session'), you'll see the reception desk in front of you (through a security barrier); the hall is through the double doors immediately on your right.

Eating

Ondine   SEAFOOD £££

15 ⊗ MAP P56, D4

Ondine is one of Edinburgh's finest seafood restaurants, with a menu based on sustainably sourced fish. Take a seat at the curved Oyster Bar and tuck into oysters with shallot dressing, shellfish bisque, lobster ther- midor, a *fruits de mer* platter or just good old haddock and chips (with minted pea puree, just to keep things posh). (☑0131-226 1888; www.ondinerestaurant.co.uk; 2 George IV Bridge; mains £22-38; ☉noon-9pm Wed-Sat, noon-4pm Sun; ☎; ☐23, 27, 41, 42)

Cannonball Restaurant   SCOTTISH ££

16 ⊗ MAP P56, B4

The historic Cannonball House next to Edinburgh Castle's

esplanade has been transformed into a sophisticated restaurant and whisky bar where the Contini family work their Italian magic on Scottish classics to produce dishes such as haggis balls with marmalade and mustard, and lobster thermidor with macaroni and cheese. (☑0131-225 1550; www. contini.com/cannonball; 356 Castlehill; mains £15-30; ☉noon-3pm & 5.30-10pm Tue-Sat; ☎⚥; ☐23, 27, 41, 42)

Mums   CAFE £

17 ⊗ MAP P56, D5

This nostalgia-fuelled cafe serves up classic British comfort food that wouldn't look out of place on a 1950s menu – bacon and eggs, bangers and mash, shepherd's pie, fish and chips. But there's a twist – the food is all top-quality nosh freshly prepared from local produce. There's also a good selection of bottled craft beers and Scottish-brewed cider. (☑0131-260 9806; www.monstermashcafe.co.uk; 4a

Old Town
History

Before the founding of the New Town in the 18th century, old Edinburgh was an overcrowded and unsanitary hive of humanity. Constrained between the boggy ground of the Nor' Loch (now drained and occupied by Princes Street Gardens) to the north and the city walls to the south and east, the only way for the town to expand was upwards.

Old Town Tenements

The five- to eight-storey tenements that were raised along the Royal Mile in the 16th and 17th centuries were the skyscrapers of their day, remarked upon with wonder by visiting writers such as Daniel Defoe. All classes of society, from beggars to magistrates, lived cheek by jowl in these urban ants nests, the wealthy occupying the middle floors – high enough to be above the noise and stink of the streets, but not so high that climbing the stairs would be too tiring – while the poor squeezed into attics, basements, cellars and vaults.

Royal Mile

The Royal Mile, Edinburgh's oldest street, connects the castle to the Palace of Holyroodhouse. It is split into four named sections: Castlehill, the Lawnmarket, the High St and the Canongate.

A corruption of 'Landmarket', **Lawnmarket** takes its name from a large cloth market (selling goods from the land outside the city) that flourished here until the 18th century; this was the poshest part of the Old Town, where many distinguished citizens made their homes.

High St, which stretches from George IV Bridge down to St Mary's St, is the heart and soul of the Old Town, home to the city's main church, the law courts, the city chambers and – until 1707 – the Scottish Parliament. The Old Town's eastern gate, the Netherbow Port (part of the Flodden Wall), once stood at the Mary's St end. Though it no longer exists, its former outline is marked by brass strips set in the road.

Canongate – the section between the Netherbow and Holyrood – takes its name from the Augustinian canons (monks) of Holyrood Abbey. From the 16th century it was home to aristocrats who wanted to live near the Palace of Holyroodhouse.

Forrest Rd; mains £9-13; 🕘9am-10pm Mon-Sat, 10am-10pm Sun; 📶👶; 🚌2, 23, 27, 35, 41, 42, 45)

Grain Store

SCOTTISH £££

18 ❌ MAP P56, C4

An atmospheric upstairs dining room on picturesque Victoria St, the Grain Store has a well-earned reputation for serving the finest Scottish produce, perfectly prepared in dishes such as halibut with fried squid and mussel bisque, and roe deer venison with celeriac, beetroot and kale. The two-course lunch for £14 is good value. (📞0131-225 7635; www.grainstore-restaurant.co.uk; 30 Victoria St; mains £24-32; 🕘noon-2.30pm & 6-9.45pm Mon-Sat, noon-2.30pm & 6-9.30pm Sun; 🚌2, 23, 27, 41, 42)

White Horse Oyster & Seafood Bar

SEAFOOD £££

19 ❌ MAP P56, G3

One of Edinburgh's oldest pubs has been transformed into this intriguing seafood restaurant. The decor is bare stone and wood panelling in shades of slate grey and brown, providing a dark canvas on which white platters of colourful shellfish and crustaceans shine all the more brightly. The menu also includes 'small plates' (£8 to £15), which can be ordered tapas-style. (📞0131-629 5300; www.whitehorseoysterbar.co.uk; 266 Canongate; seafood platters £48-95; 🕘4-10pm Mon-Fri, noon-10pm Sat & Sun; 🚌35)

Wedgwood

SCOTTISH £££

20 ❌ MAP P56, G3

Fine food without the fuss is the motto at this friendly, unpretentious restaurant. Scottish produce is served with inventive flair in mouth-watering dishes such as fillet of lamb with samphire and mint, or scallops with cauliflower korma, pineapple, and peanut and pistachio dust; the menu includes foraged wild salad leaves collected by the chef. The six-course tasting menu is £55 (vegetarian option £50). (📞0131-558 8737; www.wedgwoodtherestaurant.co.uk; 267 Canongate; mains £23-30, 2-/3-course lunch £20/25; 🕘noon-2pm Fri-Sun & 6-10pm Wed-Sun; 🍴; 🚌35)

Old Town Eating

Royal Mile

Underground Edinburgh

As Edinburgh expanded in the late 18th and early 19th centuries, new bridges were built to link the Old Town to newly developed areas to its north and south. **South Bridge** (completed 1788) and **George IV Bridge** (1834) lead southward from the Royal Mile over the deep valley of the Cowgate, but since their construction, so many buildings have clustered around them that you can hardly tell they are bridges. George IV Bridge has a total of nine arches of which only two are visible, and South Bridge has no fewer than 18 hidden arches.

These underground vaults were originally used as storerooms, workshops and drinking dens. But as early-19th-century Edinburgh's population swelled with an influx of penniless Highlanders cleared from their lands, and Irish refugees from the potato famine, the dark, dripping chambers were given over to slum accommodation. The vaults were eventually cleared in the late 19th century, then lay forgotten until 1994 when some of the South Bridge vaults were opened to guided tours (with **Mercat Tours** (Map p56, D3; ☎ 0131-225 5445; www.mercattours.com; Mercat Cross; adult/child £16/11; ⏰ 10am-9.30pm; 🚌 35)), while others are now home to atmospheric nightclubs such as Cabaret Voltaire (p68) and the Caves (p71).

Witchery by the Castle

SCOTTISH, FRENCH £££

 21 MAP P56, C4

Set in a merchant's town house dating from 1595, the Witchery is a candlelit corner of antique splendour with oak-panelled walls, low ceilings, opulent wall hangings and red-leather upholstery; stairs lead down to a second, even more romantic dining room called the Secret Garden. The menu ranges from oysters to Aberdeen Angus steak and the wine list runs to almost 1000 bins. (☎ 0131-225 5613; www.thewitchery.com; Castlehill; mains £25-44, 2-course lunch £25; ⏰ noon-11.30pm; 🚌 23, 27, 41, 42)

Scott's Kitchen

SCOTTISH, CAFE £

22 MAP P56, C4

Green tile, brown leather and arched Georgian windows lend an elegant feel to this modern cafe, which combines fine Scottish produce with international favourites. Fill up on a breakfast (served till noon) of eggs Benedict or bacon baps, or linger over a lunch of haggis bonbons, crunchy calamari or a smoked ham and Scottish cheddar sandwich. (☎ 0131-322 6868; www.scottskitchen.co.uk; 4-6 Victoria Tce; mains £8-10; ⏰ 9am-6pm; 🅿 📶; 🚌 23, 27, 41, 42)

David Bann

VEGETARIAN ££

23  MAP P56, G3

If you want to convince a carnivorous friend that cuisine à la veg can be every bit as tasty and inventive as a meat-muncher's menu, take them to David Bann's stylish restaurant – dishes such as strudel filled with mushroom, rosemary, Isle of Arran cheese and Heather Ale with polenta chips and shallot sauce are guaranteed to win converts. (☎0131-556 5888; www.davidbann.com; 56-58 St Mary's St; mains £12-15; ☺noon-10pm Mon-Fri, 11am-10pm Sat & Sun; 🖈; 🚍35)

Amber

SCOTTISH ££

(3)  MAP P56, B4

You've got to love a place where the waiter greets you with the words,

'I'll be your whisky adviser for this evening'. Located in the Scotch Whisky Experience (p58), this whisky-themed restaurant manages to avoid the tourist clichés and creates genuinely interesting and flavoursome dishes using top Scottish produce, with a suggested whisky pairing for each dish. (☎0131-477 8477; www.scotchwhiskyexperience.co.uk/restaurant; 354 Castlehill; mains £15-20; ☺11am-8pm; 🛜🚼; 🚍23, 27, 41, 42)

Wings

FAST FOOD £

24  MAP P56, E4

Eating outlets don't come much simpler. Order some bowls of barbecued chicken wings (six wings per portion) with the sauce of your choice (there are a couple of dozen to choose from, ranging

A farmers market on Lawnmarket St

from tequila and lime juice to hot chilli), and a drink. If you're still hungry, order more. Genius. Great sci-fi/comic-book decor, too. (☑0131-629 1234; www.facebook.com/wings.edinburgh; 5/7 Old Fishmarket Close; per portion £4.50; ◷4-11pm Mon, noon-11pm Tue-Sun; ☒23, 27, 41, 42)

Maxie's Bistro

BISTRO ££

25 MAP P56, C4

This candlelit bistro, with its cushion-lined nooks set amid stone walls and wooden beams, is a pleasant setting for a cosy dinner, but at summer lunchtimes people queue for the tables on the terrace overlooking Victoria St. The food is dependable, ranging from pasta, steak and stir-fries to seafood platters and daily specials. It's best to book, especially in summer. (☑0131-226 7770; www.maxiesbistro.com; 5b Johnston Tce; mains £10-27; ◷noon-11pm; 🛜👶; ☒23, 27, 41, 42, 67)

Music at St Giles

St Giles Cathedral (www.stgilescathedral.org.uk; High St, EH1 1RE; ☒23, 27, 41, 42) plays host to a regular and varied programme of classical music, including popular lunchtime and evening concerts and organ recitals. The cathedral choir sings at the 10am and 11.30am Sunday services.

Edinburgh Larder

CAFE £

26 MAP P56, F3

This bright and cheerful cafe, handily located just off the Royal Mile, puts the focus on seasonal Scottish produce (a map on the wall highlights their suppliers). Dishes range from brunch favourites such as eggs Benedict, to a Taste of Scotland platter that includes hot and cold smoked salmon, organic cheeses, oatcakes and salad leaves. (☑0131-556 2350; www.edinburghlarder.co.uk; 15 Blackfriars St; mains £9-15; ◷8am-5pm Mon, Thu & Fri, 8.30am-5pm Sat & Sun; 👶; ☒35)

Drinking

Bow Bar

PUB

27 MAP P56, C4

One of the city's best traditional-style pubs (it's not as old as it looks), serving a range of excellent real ales, Scottish craft gins and a vast selection of malt whiskies, the Bow Bar is often standing-room only on Friday and Saturday evenings. (www.thebowbar.co.uk; 80 West Bow; ◷noon-midnight; 🐾; ☒2, 23, 27, 41, 42)

Cabaret Voltaire

CLUB

28 MAP P56, E4

An atmospheric warren of stone-lined vaults houses this self-consciously 'alternative' club, which eschews huge dance floors and egotistical DJ worship in favour of a 'creative crucible' hosting an eclectic mix of DJs, live acts, comedy, theatre, visual arts and the spoken word. Well worth a look. (www.thecabaretvoltaire.com; 36-38 Blair St; ⏰5pm-3am Tue-Sat, 8pm-1am Sun; 📶; 🚌all South Bridge buses)

Bongo Club

CLUB

29 MAP P56, D4

Owned by a local arts charity, the weird and wonderful Bongo Club has a long history of hosting everything from wild club nights and local bands to performance art and kids comedy shows. (www.thebongoclub.co.uk; 66 Cowgate; ⏰11pm-3am Tue & Thu, 7pm-3am Fri-Sun; 📶; 🚌2)

BrewDog

BAR

30 🚌 MAP P56, E4

The Edinburgh outpost of Scotland's self-styled 'punk brewery', BrewDog stands out among the sticky-floored dives that line the Cowgate with its polished-concrete bar and cool, industrial-chic decor. As well as its own highly rated beers, there's a choice of guest real ales, and – a sign of a great trad pub – coat hooks under the edge of the bar. (www.brewdog.com; 143 Cowgate; ⏰noon-1am Fri-Tue, 5-10pm Wed & Thu; 📶; 🚌2, 35)

Salt Horse Beer Shop & Bar

BAR

31 🚌 MAP P56, F4

Tucked off the Royal Mile, this independent beer, food, and a shop next door selling around 400 beers to drink in or take away. Work

Pipe organ in St Giles Cathedral (p58)

your way through 12 keg lines of local and imported beers and a small but perfectly formed menu of handmade burgers, Scotch eggs, and cheese and charcuterie platters. (📞0131-558 8304; www.salthorse.beer; 57-61 Blackfriars St; ⏰4pm-midnight Mon-Fri, noon-1am Sat, 12.30pm-midnight Sun; 🚌35)

Checkpoint

BAR

32 🚌 MAP P56, E5

A friendly cafe, bar and restaurant with a comprehensive menu including breakfasts, bar bites and substantial mains, Checkpoint has gained a reputation as one of the coolest spots in Edinburgh. The utilitarian white-walled space is flooded with light from floor-to-ceiling windows and is vast enough to house, of all things, an

Sandy Bell's

Sandy Bell's (Map p56, D5; ☎0131-225 2751; 25 Forrest Rd; ⏰noon-1am Mon-Sat, 12.30pm-midnight Sun; ➡2, 23, 27, 35, 41, 42, 45) is an unassuming pub that has been a stalwart of the traditional-music scene since the 1960s (the founder's wife sang with The Corries). There's music every weekday evening at 9pm, and from 2pm Saturday and 4pm Sunday, plus lots of impromptu sessions.

old shipping container. (☎0131-225 9352; www.checkpointedinburgh.com; 3 Bristo Pl; ⏰9am-1am; 📶; ➡2, 47)

Paradise Palms   BAR

33 🅟 MAP P56, E5

If you like your student bars grungy and unpretentious, with affordable left-field cocktails (Buckfast Daiquiri, anyone?), delicious vegetarian soul food and banging music, Paradise Palms is for you. There's lots of neon, disco balls and stuffed toys hanging above the bar. Regular DJ and cabaret nights. (☎0131-225 4186; www.theparadisepalms.com; 41 Lothian St; ⏰noon-1am; 📶; ➡2, 41, 42, 47)

Holyrood 9A   PUB

34 🅟 MAP P56, G4

Candlelight flickering off hectares of polished wood creates an at-mospheric setting for this family-friendly real-ale bar, with more than 20 taps pouring craft beers from all corners of the country and indeed the globe. If you're peckish it serves excellent gourmet burgers (and there's a kids' menu). (www.theholyrood.co.uk; 9a Holyrood Rd; ⏰9am-midnight Sun-Thu, to 1am Fri & Sat; 📶♿; ➡35)

Liquid Room   CLUB

35 🅟 MAP P56, C4

Set in a subterranean vault deep beneath Victoria St, the Liquid Room is a superb club venue with a thundering sound system. There are regular club nights every Friday and Saturday, as well as DJs and live bands on other nights. Check the website for upcoming events. (www.liquidroom.com; 9c Victoria St; ⏰live music from 7pm, club nights 10.30pm-3am; ➡2, 23, 27, 41, 42)

Jolly Judge   PUB

36 🅟 MAP P56, C4

A snug little howff tucked away down a close, the Judge exudes a cosy 17th-century atmosphere (low, timber-beamed painted ceilings) and has the added attraction of a cheering open fire in cold weather. No music or gaming machines, just the buzz of conversation. (www.jollyjudge.co.uk; 7a James Ct; ⏰noon-11pm Mon-Thu, to midnight Fri & Sat, 12.30-11pm Sun; 📶; ➡23, 27, 41, 42)

Malt Shovel
PUB

37 😊 MAP P56, D3

A traditional-looking pub with dark wood and subdued tartanry, the Malt Shovel offers a good range of real ales and more than 40 malt whiskies, and serves excellent pub grub including fish and chips, burgers, and steak-and-ale pies. (☎0131-225 6843; www.maltshovelinn-edinburgh.co.uk; 11-15 Cockburn St; ⏰11am-11pm Mon-Wed, to midnight Thu & Sun, to 1am Fri & Sat; 🛜🚻; 🚌6)

Entertainment

Caves
LIVE MUSIC

38 ⭐ MAP P56, F4

A spectacular subterranean venue set in the ancient stone vaults beneath the South Bridge, the Caves stages a series of one-off club nights and live-music gigs, as well as *ceilidh* (traditional music) nights during the Edinburgh Festival. Check the What's On link on the website for upcoming events. (www.unusualvenuesedinburgh.com/venues/the-caves-venue-edinburgh; 8-12 Niddry St S; 🚌35)

Royal Oak
TRADITIONAL MUSIC

39 ⭐ MAP P56, F4

This popular folk-music pub is tiny, so get here early (9pm start weekdays, 6pm and 9.30pm sessions on Saturday, 4.30pm and 7pm sessions on Sunday) if you want to be sure of a place. Saturday night in the lounge is open session – bring your own instrument (and/or a good singing voice!). (☎0131-557 2976; www.royal-oak-folk.com; 1

The Malt Shovel Inn

Infirmary St; ⏰11.30am-2am Mon-Sat, 12.30pm-2am Sun; 🚌all South Bridge buses)

Jazz Bar

JAZZ, BLUES

40 ⭐ MAP P56, F4

This atmospheric cellar bar, with its polished parquet floors, bare stone walls, candlelit tables and stylish steel-framed chairs, is owned and operated by jazz musicians. There's live music every night from 9pm to 3am, and on Saturday from 3pm. As well as jazz, expect bands playing blues, funk, soul and fusion. (www.thejazzbar.co.uk; 1a Chambers St;

The Scotsman Steps

This is public art at its best: harmonious, understated and accessible. In 2010 Turner Prize winner Martin Creed was commissioned by the **Fruitmarket Gallery** (Map p56; E2; www.fruitmarket.co.uk; 45 Market St; admission free; ⏰11am-6pm; ♿; 🚌all North Bridge buses) to create a permanent work for Edinburgh's historic **Scotsman Steps** (Map p56; E2; www.fruitmarket.co.uk/scotsman-steps; admission free; 🚌all North Bridge buses), built in 1899 to link the Old and New Towns. Using 104 different-coloured marbles for each of the 104 steps, this elegant work has revitalised a neglected corner of the city. There are entrances on Market St and North Bridge.

£3-7; ⏰5pm-3am Sun-Fri, 1.30pm-3am Sat; 📶; 🚌35, 45)

Bannerman's

LIVE MUSIC

41 ⭐ MAP P56, F4

A long-established music venue – it seems like every Edinburgh student for the last four decades spent half their youth here – Bannerman's struggles through a warren of old vaults beneath South Bridge. It pulls in crowds of students, locals and backpackers with live rock, punk and indie bands five or six nights a week. (www.facebook.com/BannermansBar; 212 Cowgate; ⏰noon-1am Mon-Sat, 12.30pm-1am Sun; 📶; 🚌35)

Whistle Binkie's

LIVE MUSIC

42 ⭐ MAP P56, F3

This crowded cellar bar, just off the Royal Mile, has live music most nights till 3am, from rock and blues to folk and jazz. The long-standing open-mic night on Monday is a showcase for new talent. (www.whistlebinkies.com; 4-6 South Bridge; entry free, except after midnight Fri & Sat; ⏰5pm-3am Sun-Thu, 1pm-3am Fri & Sat; 🚌all South Bridge buses)

Bedlam Theatre

COMEDY

43 ⭐ MAP P56, D5

The Bedlam hosts a long-established weekly improvisation slot (running for more than 25 years), the Improverts, which is hugely popular with local students. Shows should kick off again in 2021, at 10.30pm every Friday during term time, and you're guaranteed a robust and entertaining evening. (☏0131-629 0430; www.bedlamthea tre.co.uk; 11b Bristo Pl; £3.50; ☐2, 23, 27, 41, 42)

Shopping

Armstrong's
VINTAGE

44 🔒 MAP P56, C5

Armstrong's is an Edinburgh fashion institution (established in 1840, no less), a quality vintage-clothes emporium offering everything from elegant 1940s dresses to funky 1970s flares. Aside from the retro fashion, it's a great place to hunt for preloved kilts and Harris tweed, or to seek inspiration for that fancy-dress party. (☏0131-220 5557; www.armstrongsvintage.co.uk; 83 Grassmarket; ⏰10am-5.30pm Mon-Thu, to 6pm Fri & Sat, noon-6pm Sun; ☐2)

Royal Mile Whiskies
DRINKS

45 🔒 MAP P56, D3

If it's a drap of the cratur ye're after, this place has a selection of single malts in miniature and full-size bottles. There's also a range of blended whiskies, Irish whisky and bourbon, and you can buy online, too. (☏0131-225 3383; www.royal milewhiskies.com; 379 High St; ⏰10am-6pm; ☐23, 27, 41, 42)

Bill Baber
FASHION & ACCESSORIES

46 🔒 MAP P56, C4

This family-run designer-knitwear studio has been in the business for more than 40 years, producing stylish and colourful creations using linen, merino wool, silk and cotton. (☏0131-225 3249; www.billbaber.com; 66 Grassmarket; ⏰9am-6pm Mon-Sat; ☐2)

Hannah Zakari
JEWELLERY

47 🔒 MAP P56, D4

This is Edinburgh's coolest jewellery boutique, sourcing quirky pieces by indie designers from all over the world. Necklaces, earrings, brooches, cards, art prints and accessories are gorgeously presented in a small shop that has been hit-listed in *Vogue*, *Tatler* and the *Guardian*. Pleasing to the eye, dangerous for the wallet. (☏0131-226 5433; www.hannahzakari.co.uk; 43 Candlemaker Row; ⏰noon-5.30pm Mon-Fri, 11am-5.30pm Sat, 12.30-4.30pm Sun; ☐2, 23, 27, 41, 42)

Ragamuffin
FASHION & ACCESSORIES

48 🔒 MAP P56, G3

Quality knitwear and fabrics, including cashmere from Johnstons of Elgin, Fair Isle sweaters and Harris tweed. (☏0131-557 6007; www.face book.com/ragamuffinclothesand knitwear; 278 Canongate; ⏰10am-6pm Mon-Sat, noon-5pm Sun; ☐35)

Godiva
FASHION & ACCESSORIES

49 🔒 MAP P56, B5

This unconventional, innovative boutique specialises in both vintage and modern cutting-edge designs. It has won accolades in the Scottish Variety Awards, and is committed to ethical fashion. (☎0131-221 9212; www.godivaboutique.co.uk; 9 West Port, EH1 2JA; ⏱10.30am-6pm Mon & Thu-Sat, 11.30am-5pm Sun; 🚌2)

Geoffrey (Tailor) Inc
FASHION & ACCESSORIES

50 🔒 MAP P56, F3

Geoffrey can fit you out in traditional Highland dress, or run up a kilt in your own clan tartan. The store's offshoot, **21st Century Kilts** (www.21stcenturykilts.com; based at Duntarvie Castle in West Lothian), offers modern fashion kilts in a variety of fabrics. (☎0131-557 0256; www.geoffreykilts.co.uk; 57-59 High St, EH1 1SR; ⏱9.30am-6pm Mon-Sat, 10.30am-5.30pm Sun; 🚌35)

Blackwell's Bookshop
BOOKS

51 🔒 MAP P56, F4

Oxford-based Blackwell's is the city's principal bookstore, covering all subjects, with a huge selection of academic books. (☎0131-622 8222; www.blackwell.co.uk; 53-62 South Bridge; ⏱10am-6pm Mon-Sat, noon-6pm Sun; 🚌all South Bridge buses)

Joyce Forsyth Designer Knitwear
FASHION & ACCESSORIES

52 🔒 MAP P56, D5

The colourful knitwear on show at this intriguing little shop will drag your ideas about woollens firmly into the 21st century. Ms Forsyth's trademark design is a flamboyant, flared woollen coat (it can be knitted to order in colours of your choice), but there are also

Armstrong's (p73)

SCOTT LOUDEN/SHUTTERSTOCK ©

Cockburn St Shops

Cockburn St is packed with trendy shops and boutiques where Edinburgh teens and twenty-somethings flock to browse the fashion rails. Look out for these highlights:

Pie in the Sky (Map p56, E3; ☏ 0131-220 1477; www.facebook.com/pieinthesky72; 47 Cockburn St; ⊙10am-5.30pm; ☒ 35) Vintage and alternative fashion.

Underground Solush'n (Map p56, D3; ☏ 0131-226 2242; www.undergroundsolushn.com; 9 Cockburn St; ⊙10am-5pm Mon-Wed & Sat, 10am-6pm Thu & Fri, 11am-5pm Sun; ☒ 35) New and secondhand vinyl; one of the city's best record shops.

Cookie (Map p56, E3; ☏ 0131-622 7260; www.facebook.com/cookiecockburnstreet; 29a Cockburn St; ⊙10am-5.30pm; ☒ 35) Cute party dresses.

Museum Context (Map p56, E3; ☏ 0131-629 0534; www.museumcontext.com; 42-44 Cockburn St; ⊙10am-6pm Mon-Sat, 11am-5pm Sun; ☒ 35) Aladdin's cave of unusual gifts.

box jackets, jumpers, hats, scarves and shawls. (☏ 0131-220 4112; www.joyceforsyth.co.uk; 42 Candlemaker Row; ⊙10am-5.30pm Tue-Sat; ☒ 2, 23, 27, 41, 42)

Mr Wood's Fossils
GIFTS & SOUVENIRS

53 🅐 MAP P56, C4

Founded by famous fossil hunter Stan Wood, who discovered 'Lizzie', the oldest fossil reptile yet known, this fascinating speciality shop has a wide range of minerals, gems, fossils and other geological gifts. (☏ 0131-220 1344; www.mrwoodsfos

sils.co.uk; 5 Cowgatehead; ⊙10am-5.30pm; ☒ 2)

Kilberry Bagpipes
MUSICAL INSTRUMENTS

54 🅐 MAP P56, G3

A maker and retailer of traditional Highland bagpipes, Kilberry also sells piping accessories, snare drums, books, CDs and learning materials. By appointment only during the Covid-19 pandemic. (☏ 0131-556 9607; www.kilberrybagpipes.com; 27 St Mary's St; ⊙8.30am-4.30pm Mon-Fri, 10am-2pm Sat; ☒ 35)

Explore ⟡
Holyrood &
Arthur's Seat

Facing the imposing royal palace of Holyroodhouse at the foot of the Royal Mile, a once near-derelict district has been transformed by the construction of the Scottish Parliament Building. Holyrood Park, a hunting ground of Scottish monarchs centred on the miniature mountain of Arthur's Seat, allows Edinburghers to enjoy a little bit of wilderness in the heart of the city.

The Short List

○ **Palace of Holyroodhouse (p78)** *Exploring the royal family's official residence in Scotland.*

○ **Scottish Parliament Building (p80)** *Perusing Edinburgh's most spectacular and controversial building.*

○ **Arthur's Seat (p85)** *Admiring the view from the summit of Edinburgh's mini-mountain – well worth the effort.*

○ **Rhubarb (p87)** *Getting dressed up to the nines and spoiling yourself at one of Edinburgh's most sumptuous and memorable restaurants.*

○ **Sheep Heid Inn (p88)** *Enjoying a game of bar skittles and a pint or two of craft beer in what is possibly the city's oldest pub.*

Getting There & Around

🚌 Lothian service 35 runs to Holyrood from South Bridge via the lower half of the Royal Mile. Bus 42 runs along Duddingston Rd West, a short walk from Duddingston Village, while buses 4, 5, 26, 44 and 45 run along London Rd, near the north entrance to Holyrood Park.

Neighbourhood Map on p84

MSP building, Scottish Parliament Building (p80)
ARCHITECT: ENRIC MIRALLES; CORNFIELD/SHUTTERSTOCK ©

Top Sight 📸
Palace of Holyroodhouse

◎ MAP P84, B2

The Palace of Holyroodhouse is the royal family's official residence in Scotland, but it is probably most famous as the home of the ill-fated Mary, Queen of Scots. She spent six turbulent years here from 1561 to 1567, during which time she debated with John Knox, married her second and third husbands, and witnessed the murder of her secretary David Rizzio.

www.rct.uk/visit/palace-of-holyroodhouse

Canongate, Royal Mile

adult/child incl audio guide £16.50/9.50

🕓 9.30am-6pm, last entry 4.30pm Apr-Oct, to 4.30pm, last entry 3.15pm Nov-Mar

🚌 35

Great Gallery

A self-guided audio tour leads you through a series of impressive royal apartments, ending in the **Great Gallery**. The 89 portraits of Scottish kings (both real and legendary) were commissioned by Charles II and supposedly record his unbroken lineage from Scota, the Egyptian pharaoh's daughter who discovered the infant Moses in a reed basket on the banks of the Nile.

Mary's Bedchamber

The highlight of the tour is a bedchamber that was home to the unfortunate Mary, Queen of Scots (it's connected to her husband's bedchamber by a **secret stairway**). It was here that her jealous second husband, Lord Darnley, restrained the pregnant queen while his henchmen murdered her secretary – and favourite – David Rizzio; a plaque in the neighbouring room marks the spot where he bled to death.

Holyrood Abbey

Admission to the palace includes a guided tour of neighbouring **Holyrood Abbey** (www.histori cenvironment.scot; Canongate, EH8 8DX; free with Palace of Holyroodhouse; April to October only), founded by David I in 1128. It was probably named after a fragment of the True Cross, on which Christ was crucified (*rood* is an old Scots word for cross), said to have been brought back from the Holy Land by his mother, St Margaret. Most of the surviving ruins date from the 12th and 13th centuries; the royal burial vault holds the remains of David II, James II and James V, and Lord Darnley, husband of Mary, Queen of Scots.

★ Top Tips

o The palace is closed to the public when the royal family is visiting and during state functions (usually in mid-May, and mid-June to early July); check the website for dates.

o You can wander through the palace at your own speed; an audio guide is included in the price of admission. Allow at least one to 1½ hours.

o If you plan to visit the Queen's Gallery (p86) as well, you can buy a combined ticket.

✗ Take a Break

o The **Café at the Palace** (Mews Courtyard, Queen's Gallery, Horse Wynd, EH8 8DX; mains £6-11; ⏰9.30am-6pm Apr-Oct, to 4.30pm Nov-Mar; 👶; 🚌35), in the courtyard of the Queen's Gallery, serves soup and snacks.

o Hemma (p88) is a short walk away, and does family-friendly food.

Top Sight 📷
Scottish Parliament Building

The Scottish Parliament Building is a spectacular example of modern architecture, designed by Catalan architect Enric Miralles and officially opened by the Queen in 2004. It's an original and idiosyncratic building that caused a great deal of controversy at the time but now provides a home for the parliament created in the wake of the Scottish devolution referendum of 1997.

🎯 MAP P84, B2

www.parliament.scot

Horse Wynd,

admission free

🕐 9am-6.30pm Tue-Thu, 10am-5pm Mon, Fri & Sat in session, 10am-5pm Tue-Thu in recess

🚌 35

The Exterior

Architect Enric Miralles (1955–2000) believed that a building could be a work of art. However, this weird concrete confection has left many people scratching their heads in confusion. What does it all mean? The strange forms of the exterior are each symbolic in some way, from the oddly shaped projecting windows on the western wall (inspired by the silhouette of *The Reverend Robert Walker Skating on Duddingston Loch,* one of Scotland's most famous paintings) to the unusual, inverted-L-shaped panels on the facade (representing a curtain being drawn aside, ie open government). The ground plan of the whole complex represents a 'flower of democracy rooted in Scottish soil' (best seen looking down from Salisbury Crags).

The Debating Chamber

The **Main Hall**, inside the public entrance, has a low, triple-arched ceiling of polished concrete, like a cave, or cellar, or castle vault. It is a dimly lit space, the starting point for a metaphorical journey from this relative darkness up to the **Debating Chamber** (sitting directly above the Main Hall), which is, in contrast, a palace of light – the light of democracy. This magnificent chamber is the centrepiece of the parliament, designed not to glorify but to humble the politicians who sit within it. The windows face Calton Hill, allowing members of the Scottish parliament (MSPs) to look up to its monuments (reminders of the Scottish Enlightenment), while the massive, pointed oak beams of the roof are suspended by steel threads above the MSPs' heads like so many Damoclean swords.

★ **Top Tips**

o The public areas of the parliament building – the Main Hall, where there is an exhibition, a shop and cafe, and the public gallery in the Debating Chamber. Tickets are needed for the public gallery – see the website for details.

o You can also take a free, one-hour guided tour (advance bookings recommended).

o If you want to see the parliament in session, check the website for sitting times – business days are normally Tuesday to Thursday year-round.

✗ **Take a Break**

o There is a cafe in the Parliament Building at the rear of the Main Hall.

o Another cafe is across the street in the Queen's Gallery.

Walking Tour 🥾

A Walk Through Holyrood Park

Holyrood Park covers 263 hectares of varied landscape, including crags, moorland and lochs, plus the miniature mountain of Arthur's Seat, little changed since its enclosure as a royal hunting ground in the 16th century. It's a wildlife haven and a huge recreational resource for the city, thronged with walkers, cyclists and picnickers on sunny weekends.

Walk Facts

Start Holyrood Park, northern entrance; bus: Meadowbank Stadium

Finish Duddingston Village; bus: Holyrood High School

Length 2.6 miles; two hours

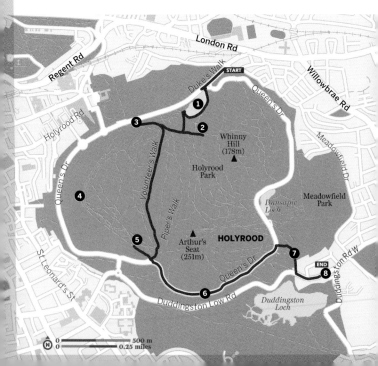

❶ St Margaret's Loch

Begin at the park's northern entrance on Duke's Walk, which leads to St Margaret's Loch. It's well known for its huge flocks of swans and ducks (don't feed them – human food isn't healthy for wild animals).

❷ St Anthony's Chapel

Take the path on the south side of the loch and climb up to St Anthony's Chapel's ruins. Its origins are obscure; it may have been associated with a hospital in Leith donated by King James I (to treat the skin disease erysipelas, aka St Anthony's Fire), or may have been a beacon for ships in the Firth of Forth.

❸ St Margaret's Well

Descend back to the road where you'll find St Margaret's Well, a beautiful, late-15th-century Gothic well house. It was moved to this location in 1860, when its original Meadowbank site was taken over by a railway depot. Peek at the ornate vaulting through the metal grille at the entrance.

❹ Radical Road

The path along the foot of Salisbury Crags is known as the Radical Road – it was built in 1820, at Sir Walter Scott's suggestion, to give work to unemployed weavers (from whose politics it took its name). It's closed due to the danger of rockfall: retrace your steps and fork right along Volunteer's Walk instead.

❺ Hutton's Section

At the southern end of the crags, look for an interpretation board set in a boulder marking Hutton's Section. Edinburgh's most famous rock outcrop was used by the geologist James Hutton in 1788 to bolster his theory that the Salisbury Crags' basaltic rocks were formed by molten lava cooling.

❻ Queen's Drive

Continue onto Queen's Dr, a 19th-century scenic carriage drive for Queen Victoria and Prince Albert. Closed to cars on Sundays, the drive winds across Arthur's Seat's southern slopes, with grand views over the city to the Pentland Hills.

❼ Jacob's Ladder

Where the road curves sharply to the north (left), a (signposted) footpath on the right leads to Jacob's Ladder, a steep staircase (209 steps) that descends to Duddingston Village's western edge.

❽ Duddingston Village

Picturesque Duddingston dates from the 12th century, though only the church survives from that era; most of the houses were built in the 18th century, including the village pub, the Sheep Heid Inn (p88), a good place to stop for lunch or a pint. Nearby is **Prince Charlie's Cottage**, where the Young Pretender held a council of war before the 1745 Battle of Prestonpans.

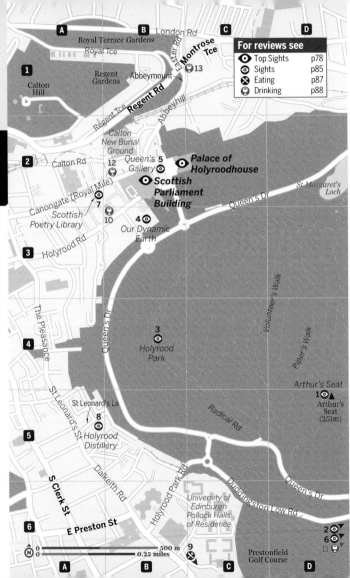

For reviews see
- ◉ Top Sights p78
- ◉ Sights p85
- ✕ Eating p87
- ☐ Drinking p88

Sights

Arthur's Seat

VIEWPOINT

1 ◎ MAP P84, D5

The rocky peak of Arthur's Seat (251m), carved by ice sheets from the deeply eroded stump of a long-extinct volcano, is a distinctive feature of Edinburgh's skyline. The view from the summit is well worth the walk, extending from the Forth bridges in the west to the distant conical hill of North Berwick Law in the east, with the Ochil Hills and the Highlands on the northwestern horizon. You can hike from Holyrood to the summit in around 45 minutes. (Holyrood Park; 🚌35)

Dr Neil's Garden

GARDENS

2 ◎ MAP P84, D6

Edinburgh's quintessential secret garden, in the shadow of a 12th-century kirk, is one of the most peaceful green spaces in Scotland. Cultivated in the 1960s by doctors Andrew and Nancy Neil from a scrappy piece of wilderness where Arthur's Seat slopes down to Duddingston Loch, the planting is a mixture of conifers, heathers and alpines, with a remarkable physic garden. Seek out a bench and soak up the meditative atmosphere of this special place. (📞07849 187995; www.drneilsgarden.co.uk; Old Church Lane, Duddingston Village; admission free; 🕙10am-dusk; 🚌42)

Dr Neil's Garden

Urban Hillwalking on Arthur's Seat

To climb Arthur's Seat from Holyrood, cross Queen's Dr and follow the path that slants leftward up the hillside from the north end of Salisbury Crags, heading towards the ruins of St Anthony's Chapel, then turn south on a rough path that follows the floor of a shallow dip just east of Long Row crags. The path eventually curves around to the left and rises more steeply up some steps to a saddle; turn right here and climb to the rocky summit of Arthur's Seat.

Holyrood Park
PARK

3 ⊙ MAP P84, B4

In Holyrood Park Edinburgh is blessed with a little bit of wilderness in the heart of the city. The former hunting ground of Scottish monarchs, the park covers 263 hectares of varied landscape, including crags, moorland and loch, and the 251m summit of Arthur's Seat (p85). Holyrood Park can be circumnavigated by car or bike along Queen's Dr. (🚌6, 35)

Our Dynamic Earth
MUSEUM

4 ⊙ MAP P84, B3

Housed in a modernistic white marquee, Our Dynamic Earth is an interactive, multimedia journey of discovery through Earth's history from the Big Bang to the present day. Hugely popular with kids of all ages, it's a slick extravaganza of whiz-bang special effects and 3D movies cleverly designed to fire young minds with curiosity about all things geological and environmental. Its true purpose, of course, is to disgorge you into a gift shop where you can buy toy dinosaurs and souvenir T-shirts. (www.dynamicearth.co.uk; Holyrood Rd; adult/child £15.95/9.95; ⏱10am-5.30pm Easter-Oct, to 6pm Jul & Aug, 10am-5.30pm Wed-Sun Nov-Easter; 👫; 🚌35)

Queen's Gallery
GALLERY

5 ⊙ MAP P84, B2

This stunning modern gallery, which occupies the shell of a former church and school, is a showcase for exhibitions of art from the Royal Collections. The exhibitions change every six months or so; for current details, check the website. (www.rct.uk/visit/the-queens-gallery-palace-of-holyroodhouse; Horse Wynd; adult/child £7.80/3.90, with Holyroodhouse £21.90/12; ⏱9.30am-6pm, last entry 4.30pm Apr-Oct, to 4.30pm, last entry 3.15pm Nov-Mar; 🚌35)

Duddingston Kirk
CHURCH

6 ⊙ MAP P84, D6

Poised on a promontory overlooking Duddingston Loch, this church is one of the oldest buildings in Edinburgh, with some interesting medieval relics at the kirkyard gate: the **Joug**, a metal collar that was used, like the stocks, to tether criminals and sinners, and the **Loupin-On Stane**, a stone step to help gouty and corpulent parishioners get onto their horses. The early 19th-century **watch-tower** inside the gate was built to deter body snatchers (p61). (www.duddingstonkirk.co.uk; Old Church Lane, Duddingston Village; admission free; ⊙10am-4pm Thu-Sat, 1-4pm Wed & Sun; 🚌42)

Scottish Poetry Library
MUSEUM

 7 MAP P84, A2

A fantastic literary resource housed in award-winning modern architecture off Canongate, the poetry library hosts regular exhibitions and is a source of information on the mysterious Edinburgh Book Sculptures (p114). (☎0131-557 2876; www.spl.org.uk; 5 Crichton's Cl; admission free; ⊙10am-5pm Tue-Fri, to 4pm Sat; 🚌35)

Holyrood Distillery
DISTILLERY

8 ⊙ MAP P84, A5

Opened in 2019 and housed in a 180-year-old railway engine shed, this is the first operating distillery in Edinburgh since 1925 (another is planned for Leith). It's too new for its whisky to be available yet (that takes at least three years), but the guided tour takes you through the spirit-making process and offers the chance to taste whiskies from other distilleries. (☎0131-285 8977; www.holyrood distillery.co.uk; 19 St Leonards Lane, EH8 9SH; tours £16.50; ⊙noon-6pm Thu-Sun; 🚌14)

Eating

Rhubarb
SCOTTISH £££

9 ✖ MAP P84, C6

Set in the splendid 17th-century **Prestonfield Hotel** (☎0131-668 3346; www.prestonfield.com; Priestfield Rd; r/ste from £355/445; P 🛜 🐾), Rhubarb is a feast for the eyes as well as the taste buds. The over-the-top decor of rich reds set off

---

Edinburgh's Mysterious Book Sculptures

In 2011 and 2012 an unknown artist left a series of intricate and beautiful paper sculptures in various Edinburgh libraries, museums and bookshops (more sculptures appeared in 2013 and 2014). Each was fashioned from an old book and alluded to literary themes; a message from the anonymous artist revealed they had been inspired by the poem 'Gifts', by Edinburgh poet Norman MacCaig. Two are on display at the **Scottish Poetry Library**, where you can pick up a self-guided walking-tour leaflet, *Gifted: The Edinburgh Book Sculptures*.

with black and gold and sensuous surfaces – damask, brocade, marble and gilded leather – are matched by the intense flavours and rich textures of the modern Scottish cuisine. Vegetarian and vegan menus available.

Take your postprandial coffee and brandy upstairs to the sumptuous fireside sofas in the Tapestry and Leather rooms. A two-/three-course lunch menu is available for £27/33. (☏0131-225 1333; www.prestonfield. com/dine/rhubarb; Prestonfield, Priestfield Rd; mains £23-40; ⏱noon-8pm; P✍)

Drinking

Hemma   BAR

10 🍺 MAP P84, B3

Set among the glass-and-steel architecture of the redeveloped Holyrood district, Hemma (Swedish for 'at home') is one of a stable of Scandinavian bars, a funky fish tank of a place furnished with comfy armchairs and sofas and brightly coloured wooden chairs. Good coffee and cakes during the day; real ale and cocktails in the evening. (☏0131-629 3327; www. bodabar.com/hemma; 75 Holyrood Rd; ⏱11am-8pm Mon, to 11pm Tue & Wed, to midnight Thu, to 1am Fri & Sat, 10am-8pm Sun; 🛜♿; 🖳35)

Sheep Heid Inn   PUB

11 🍺 MAP P84, D6

Possibly the oldest inn in Edinburgh (with a licence dating back to 1360), the Sheep Heid feels more like an upmarket country pub than an Edinburgh bar. Set in the semirural shadow of Arthur's Seat (p85), it's famous for its 19th-

---

Mystery of the Miniature Coffins

In July 1836 some boys hunting for rabbits on the slopes of Arthur's Seat made a strange discovery: in a hollow beneath a rock, arranged on a pile of slates, were 17 tiny wooden coffins. Each was just four inches (10cm) long and contained a roughly carved human figure dressed in handmade clothes.

Many theories have been put forward in explanation, but the most convincing is that the coffins were made in response to the infamous Burke and Hare murders: the number of coffins matched the number of known victims. It was a common belief that people whose bodies had been dissected by anatomists could not enter heaven, and it is thought that someone fashioned the tiny figures in order to provide the murder victims with a form of Christian burial.

Eight of the 17 coffins survive, and can be seen in the National Museum of Scotland (p48). Edinburgh author Ian Rankin makes use of the story of the coffins in his detective novel *The Falls*.

Scottish Poetry Library (p87)

century skittles alley and its lovely little beer garden. (www.thesheep heidedinburgh.co.uk; 43-45 The Causeway, EH15 3QA; ⏰11am-11pm Mon-Thu, to midnight Fri & Sat, noon-11pm Sun; 👫🏻; 🚌42)

Kilderkin

PUB

12 🚇 MAP P84, B2

A successful attempt at reinventing the local neighbourhood pub, with polished mahogany, stained glass and snug booths, the Kilderkin stages regular community-building events such as quizzes, openmic evenings, ukulele nights and whisky-tasting sessions. The bar serves hand-pulled pints of cask ale, more than 100 varieties of rum, and decent food. (📞0131-556 2101; www.kilderkin.co.uk; 67 Canongate; ⏰11am-midnight Mon-Fri, to 1am Sat, 12.30-8pm Sun; 📶👫🏻; 🚌35)

Regent

PUB, GAY

13 🚇 MAP P84, C1

This is a pleasant gay local with a relaxed atmosphere (no loud music) that serves coffee and croissants as well as excellent real ales, including Deuchars IPA and Caledonian 80/-. It's the meeting place for various community groups including Bear Scots (second Saturday of the month) and the Ruby Fruits (first Sunday of the month). (📞0131-661 8198; 2 Montrose Tce; ⏰noon-1am Mon-Sat, 12.30pm-1am Sun; 🏻; 🚌35)

Explore ◎
New Town

Edinburgh's New Town is the world's most complete and unspoilt example of Georgian architecture and town planning; along with the Old Town, it was declared a Unesco World Heritage Site in 1995. Princes St is one of Britain's most spectacular shopping streets, with unbroken views of the castle, while George St is lined with designer boutiques, trendy bars and upmarket restaurants.

The Short List

∘ **Scottish National Portrait Gallery (p92)** *Exploring Scottish history by means of portraits of famous characters.*

∘ **Princes Street Gardens (p94)** *Wandering through one of Britain's most dramatically situated city parks.*

∘ **New Town shopping (98)** *Searching for that something special in the gorgeous boutiques on Thistle St.*

∘ **Scott Monument (p95)** *Climbing the 287 stairs to the top of this soaring neo-Gothic monument to soak up the views.*

∘ **Café Royal Circle Bar (p111)** *Sipping a pint of IPA (India pale ale) in one of Edinburgh's finest Victorian pubs.*

Getting There & Around

🚌 Just about every bus service in Edinburgh runs along Princes St at some point in its journey, but note that not all buses stop at every bus stop – if you're looking for a particular bus, check the route numbers listed on the bus-stop sign.

🚊 The tram line runs from the West End along Princes St to York Pl.

Neighbourhood Map on p100

Calton Hill (p103) ANNA KUCHEROVA /SHUTTERSTOCK ©

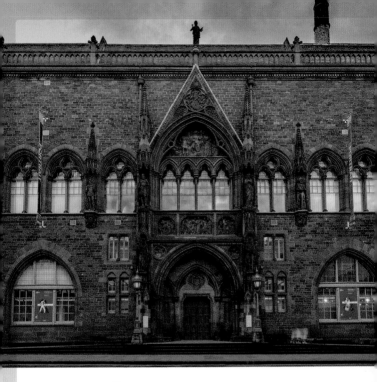

Top Sight 📷
Scottish National Portrait Gallery

The renovated Venetian Gothic palace of the Scottish National Portrait Gallery is one of the city's top attractions. Its many and varied galleries illustrate Scottish history through paintings, photographs and sculptures, putting faces to Scotland's famous names, from Robert Burns, Mary, Queen of Scots, and Bonnie Prince Charlie to the late Sir Sean Connery, comedian Billy Connolly and poet Jackie Kay.

◉ MAP P100, E3

✆ 0131-624 6200

www.nationalgalleries.org

1 Queen St

admission free

🕑 10am-5pm

🚹

🚌 all York Pl buses, 🚇 St Andrew Sq

Architecture

The museum's exterior is a neo-Gothic froth of friezes, pinnacles and sculptures – the niches at 1st-floor level hold statues of Scottish kings and queens, philosophers and poets, artists and scientists. Mary, Queen of Scots, is in the middle of the east wall on North St Andrew St, while the main entrance is framed by Robert the Bruce and William Wallace.

Great Hall

The gallery's interior is decorated in Arts and Crafts style, nowhere more splendidly than in the Great Hall. Above the Gothic colonnade a processional frieze painted by William Hole in 1898 serves as a 'visual encyclopedia' of famous Scots, shown in chronological order from Calgacus (the chieftain who led the Caledonian tribes into battle against the Romans) to writer and philosopher Thomas Carlyle (1795–1881). The murals on the 1st-floor balcony depict scenes from Scottish history, while the ceiling is painted with the constellations of the night sky.

Bonnie Prince Charlie

Contrast the 1750 portrait of a dashing Prince Charles Edward Stuart (1720–88), in tartan suit and Jacobite bonnet, at a time when he still had hopes of returning to Scotland to claim the throne, with the one painted towards the end of his life – exiled in Rome, an alcoholic and a broken man.

Three Oncologists

This eerie portrait by Ken Currie of three leading cancer specialists somehow captures the horror of the disease along with the sense that their achievements in treating it are a kind of alchemical mystery.

★ Top Tips

o The gallery's selection of 'trails' leaflets provide a bit of background information while leading you around the various exhibits; the Hidden Histories trail is particularly interesting.

o Free guided tours of the gallery's architecture are held at 2pm on the third Saturday of the month; book in advance by calling 0131-624 6560.

✕ Take a Break

o The excellent soups and sandwiches at the gallery's **Cafe Portrait** (☎0131-558 7031; www.heritage portfolio.co.uk/cafes/ our-cafes/cafe-portrait; 1 Queen St; mains £7-11; ⊙10am-4.30pm; 🛜; 🚇St Andrew Sq) make it a popular lunch spot for local office workers.

o If that's too crowded, head a block west and south to the Dome (p108) for top nosh in a stunning setting.

Top Sight 📷
Princes Street Gardens

The beautiful Princes Street Gardens are slung between Edinburgh's Old and New Towns, and split in two by the Mound – around two million cartloads of earth that were dug out from foundations during the construction of the New Town and dumped here to provide a road link across the valley to the Old Town. The road was completed in 1830.

⊙ MAP P100, B6

Princes St

admission free

⊙ dawn-dusk

🚌 all Princes St buses,
🚋 Princes St

Scott Monument

The eastern half of Princes Street Gardens is dominated by the massive Gothic spire of the **Scott Monument** (www.edinburghmuseums.org. uk; East Princes Street Gardens; tours £6; ☾10am-4pm), built by public subscription in memory of novelist Sir Walter Scott after his death in 1832. The exterior is decorated with carvings of characters from his novels; inside you can see an exhibition on Scott's life, and climb the 287 steps to the top for a superb view of the city.

West End Churches

The western end of the gardens is dominated by the tower of **St John's Church** (Princes St, EH1 2AB), worth visiting for its fine Gothic Revival interior. It overlooks **St Cuthbert's Parish Church** (Lothian Rd; ▢all Lothian Rd buses), built in the 1890s on a site of great antiquity – there has been a church here since at least the 12th century, and perhaps since the 7th century. There's a circular **watchtower** in the graveyard, a reminder of the days when graves had to be guarded against body snatchers (p61).

Floral Clock & Ross Bandstand

At the entrance to the western gardens on the corner of Princes St and the Mound is the **Floral Clock**, a working clock laid out in flowers whose deisgn changes every year; it was first created in 1903. In the middle of the western part of the gardens is the **Ross Bandstand**, a venue for open-air concerts in summer and at Hogmanay, and the stage for the famous fireworks concert during the Edinburgh International Festival (there are plans to replace the ageing bandstand with a modern concert venue).

★ Top Tips

o The gardens are home to events throughout the year, from the Edinburgh International Festival's fireworks concert to the Christmas Market and Ferris wheel in December.

o Spring is the time to see the flower displays at their best – in April the slopes below the castle esplanade are thick with yellow daffodils.

o On Saturday you can buy food from the farmers' market on Castle Tce, then grab a bench in the neighbouring gardens for an al fresco meal.

✕ Take a Break

The Scottish Cafe & Restaurant (p110), beneath the Royal Scottish Academy, offers the chance to enjoy traditional Scottish cuisine with a view along the eastern gardens.

New Town Princes Street Gardens

Walking Tour 🥾

Charlotte Square to Calton Hill

Edinburgh's New Town is one of the world's finest Georgian cityscapes, well worthy of its Unesco World Heritage status. This walk captures the essence of the New Town's Georgian elegance, taking in its two architecturally pivotal squares, the grand town houses of Heriot Row (complete with private gardens), and two of the city's best viewpoints, the Scott Monument and Calton Hill.

Walk Facts

Start Charlotte Sq; bus: Queensferry St

Finish Calton Hill; bus: St Andrew's House

Length 1.5 miles; one hour

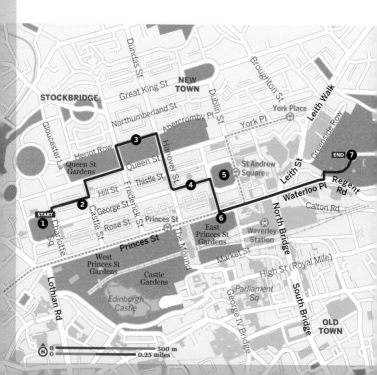

❶ Charlotte Square

Charlotte Square (p102) is a masterpiece of neoclassical design. On the north side is the museum Georgian House (p102), while off the southeast corner is **16 South Charlotte St**, birthplace of telephone pioneer Alexander Graham Bell.

❷ Oxford Bar

Leave the square at its northeast corner and turn right along Young St, passing the Oxford Bar (p112), made famous by Ian Rankin's Inspector Rebus novels. Turn left on N Castle St, right on Queen St then left again, taking a peek into the private **Queen Street Gardens**.

❸ Heriot Row

Turn right into Heriot Row, a typically elegant New Town terrace. At No 17 an inscription marks the house where writer Robert Louis Stevenson spent his childhood. It's said that the island in the pond in Queen Street Gardens (not open to the public) was the inspiration for *Treasure Island*.

❹ George Street

Go uphill to George St and turn left. This was once the centre of Edinburgh's financial industry; now the banks and offices have been taken over by designer boutiques and cocktail bars. Pop into the **Dome Grill Room** at No 14, formerly a bank, to see the ornate Georgian banking hall.

❺ St Andrew Square

The New Town's most impressive square is dominated by the **Melville Monument**, commemorating Henry Dundas (1742–1811), the most powerful Scottish politician of his time. On the far side is **Dundas House**, a Palladian mansion that houses the head office of the Royal Bank of Scotland (another magnificent domed banking hall lies within).

❻ Scott Monument

South St David St leads past Jenners (p117), the grand dame of Edinburgh department stores, to the Scott Monument (p95). Climb the 287 steps to the top for an incomparable view over Princes Street Gardens (p94) to the castle.

❼ Calton Hill

Head east along Princes St and Waterloo Pl to the stairs on the left, just after the side street called Calton Hill. Climb to the summit of Calton Hill (p103), one of Edinburgh's finest viewpoints, with a panorama that stretches from the Firth of Forth to the Pentland Hills.

Walking Tour 🥾

Hit the Shops in New Town

Shopping in the New Town offers everything from mall-crawling and traditional department stores to browsing in dinky little designer boutiques and rubbing shoulder bags with fussing fashionistas in Harvey Nicks. And all in a compact city centre that you can cover without blowing the bank on taxis or getting blisters from your Blahniks.

Walk Facts

Start Princes St; tram: Princes St

Finish St Andrew Sq; tram: St Andrew Sq

Length 1.5 miles; one hour

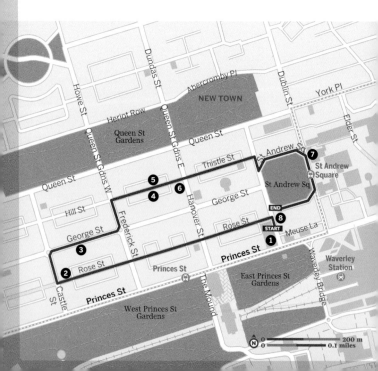

❶ Jenners

Founded in 1838, Jenners (p117) is the grande dame of Edinburgh shopping. Its five floors stock a wide range of quality goods, both classic and contemporary (it's especially strong on designer shoes and handbags, hats, knitwear and Asian rugs), and there's a food hall, hairdresser, gift-wrapping service and four cafes.

❷ Rose Street

Pedestrianised Rose St was once notorious as a pub crawl; there are still pubs, but the street is better known today for shops, mostly mainstream, which range from outdoor-sports emporiums such as Cotswold Outdoor and Tiso to silver jewellery specialists like Perre (p116).

❸ Cruise

An ornately corniced foyer leads into three floors of minimalist gallery-like decor. This **Cruise** branch at 94 George St and an outlet at nearby No 80 show off the best of mainstream designer labels including Paul Smith, Jasper Conran, Hugo Boss, Joseph Tricot, Armani and Dolce & Gabbana.

❹ Jane Davidson

Thistle St, Rose St's partner to the north of George St, has become an enclave of designer boutiques. Jane Davidson (52 Thistle St) offers luxury fashion brands such as Diane von Furstenberg, Huishan Zhang, Dries Van Noten and Queene and Belle, plus Brodie cashmere and Nanushka vegan leather.

❺ Alchemia

Made in a workshop in Fife, the jewellery on display at Alchemia (p116) is designed in Scotland and inspired by the shapes and colours of the natural world. You can also request bespoke jewellery – former clients have included royalty.

❻ Covet

Another Thistle St stalwart, at No 20, **Covet** has an emphasis on up-and-coming new designers from all over the world. Look for bags by Dutch label Smaak and New York designer Rebecca Minkoff, Tatty Devine jewellery and Triwa watches.

❼ Harvey Nichols

Harvey Nichols (p117) has four floors of designer labels and is the anchor for the Multrees Walk luxury shopping mall. Nearby you'll find Louis Vuitton, Mulberry, Hugo Boss and Swarovski boutiques.

❽ Ivy on the Square

By now you'll be looking forward to a break; The Ivy on the Square (p109) is an ideal place for lunch, or perhaps a self-indulgent afternoon tea.

New Town

For reviews see

◉ Top Sights p92
◎ Sights p102
✖ Eating p105
🍷 Drinking p111
★ Entertainment p113
🛍 Shopping p115

Edinburgh
Academy

King
George V
Park

Henderson Row

Eyre Pl

Royal Cres

Scotland St

Fettes Row

Cumberland St

Drummond
Pl

Dundonald St

35 🍷

37 🍷

Hamilton Pl

Clarence St

St Stephen St

St Vincent St

Circus La

Great King St

Kerr St

NW Circus Pl

Circus Pl

Howe St

Dundas St

Northumberland St

India Pl

India St

Royal Circus

Dean
Gardens

Gloucester La

Jamaica Mews

Heriot Row

Abercromby Pl

🛍 **46**

Moray Pl

Queen St
Gdns W

Queen St
Gdns E

Queen St
Gardens

Queen St

33 ✖
18

Thistle St

24 ✖ **25** ✖ **48** 🛍

🍷 **30**

26 ✖

George St

21 ✖ **34**

55 🛍 🍷

Rose St

St Colme St

Queen St

N Castle St

Hill St

Hanover St

Young St

🍷 **36**

✖✖ **23**

28

Frederick St

St Charlotte St

3 Georgian
◉ House

38 🍷

47 🛍

49 🛍

George St

Castle St

Princes St

🍷 **2** Royal
◉ Scottish
Academy

The Mound

4 ◉
Charlotte
Square

🛍 **15**

Rose St

Princes St

◉ **1**
Scottish
National Gallery

Hope St

Princes St

Princes Street
Gardens

West Princes St
Gardens

Lothian Rd

🛍 **51**

Edinburgh
Castle

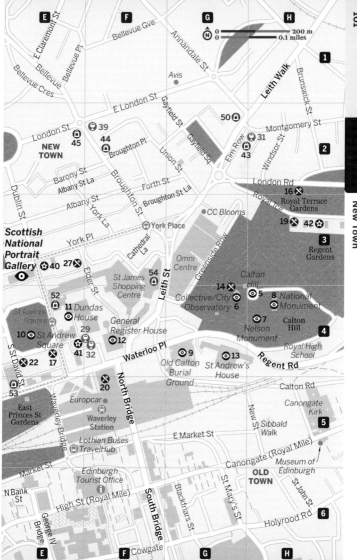

Sights

Scottish National Gallery

GALLERY

1 ◉ MAP P100, D5

Designed by William Playfair, this imposing classical building with its Ionic porticoes dates from 1850. Its octagonal rooms, lit by skylights, have been restored to their original Victorian decor of deep-green carpets and dark-red walls. The gallery houses an important collection of European art from the Renaissance to the post-Impressionism era, with works by Verrocchio (Leonardo da Vinci's teacher), Tintoretto, Titian, Holbein, Rubens, van Dyck, Vermeer, El Greco, Poussin, Rembrandt, Gainsborough, Turner, Constable, Monet, Pissarro, Gauguin and Cézanne. (📞0131-624 6200; www.nationalgalleries.org; The Mound; admission free; 🕙10am-5pm Fri-Wed, to 7pm Thu; 🚌all Princes St buses, 🚊Princes St)

Royal Scottish Academy

GALLERY

2 ◉ MAP P100, D5

This Greek Doric temple, with its northern pediment crowned by a seated figure of Queen Victoria, is the home of the Royal Scottish Academy. Designed by William Playfair and built between 1823 and 1836, it was originally called the Royal Institution; the RSA took over the building in 1910. The galleries display a collection of paintings, sculptures and architectural

drawings by academy members from 1831 on, and they host temporary exhibitions throughout the year (fees for these vary). (📞0131-225 6671; www.royalscottishacademy.org; The Mound; admission free; 🕙10am-5pm Mon-Sat, noon-5pm Sun; 🚌all Princes St buses, 🚊Princes St)

Georgian House

HISTORIC BUILDING

3 ◉ MAP P100, A5

The National Trust for Scotland's Georgian House has been beautifully restored and furnished to show how Edinburgh's wealthy elite lived at the end of the 18th century. The walls are decorated with paintings by Allan Ramsay, Sir Henry Raeburn and Sir Joshua Reynolds, and there's a fully equipped 18th-century kitchen complete with china closet and wine cellar. (NTS; www.nts.org.uk; 7 Charlotte Sq; adult/child £8/6; 🕙10am-5pm Apr-Oct, 11am-4pm Mar & Nov, closed Dec-Feb; 🚌19, 36, 37, 41, 47)

Charlotte Square

SQUARE

4 ◉ MAP P100, A5

At the western end of George St is Charlotte Sq, the architectural jewel of the New Town, which was designed by Robert Adam shortly before his death in 1791. The northern side of the square is Adam's masterpiece and one of the finest examples of Georgian architecture anywhere. **Bute House** (6 Charlotte Sq), in the centre at No 6, is the official residence of Scotland's first minister. (🚌19, 36, 37, 41, 47)

Calton Hill

VIEWPOINT

5  MAP P100, H4

Calton Hill (100m), which rises dramatically above the eastern end of Princes St, is Edinburgh's acropolis, its summit scattered with grandiose memorials dating mostly from the first half of the 19th century. It is also one of the best viewpoints in Edinburgh, with a panorama that takes in the castle, Holyrood, Arthur's Seat, the Firth of Forth, the New Town and the full length of Princes St. (🚌 104, 113, 124)

Collective/City Observatory

GALLERY

6  MAP P100, G4

The design of the City Observatory, built in 1818, was based on the Temple of the Winds in Athens.

Its original function was to provide a precise, astronomical timekeeping service for marine navigators, but smoke from Waverley train station forced the astronomers to move to Blackford Hill in the south of Edinburgh in 1895. The observatory has been redeveloped as a stunning space for contemporary visual art, and opened to the public for the first time in its history. (🖉 0131-556 1264; www.collective gallery.net; Calton Hill; admission free; 🕙 10am-5pm Tue-Sun Apr-Jul & Sep, to 4pm Oct-Mar, to 6pm daily Aug; 🚌 104, 113, 124)

Nelson Monument

MONUMENT

7  MAP P100, H4

Looking a bit like an upturned telescope – the similarity is intentional – and offering superb views over

Collective/City Observatory

4KCLIPS/SHUTTERSTOCK ©

the city and across the Firth of Forth, the Nelson Monument was built to commemorate Admiral Lord Nelson's victory at Trafalgar in 1805. (www.edinburgh museums.org.uk; Calton Hill; £6; ☺10am-7pm Mon-Sat, noon-5pm Sun Apr-Sep, 10am-4pm Mon-Sat Oct-Mar; 🚌104, 113, 124)

National Monument MONUMENT

8 ◉ MAP P100, H4

The largest structure on the summit of Calton Hill, the National Monument was a rather over-ambitious attempt to replicate the Parthenon in Athens, and was intended to honour Scotland's dead in the Napoleonic Wars. Paid for by public subscription construction began in 1822, but funds ran dry after only 12 columns had been erected. It became known locally as 'Edinburgh's Disgrace'. (Calton Hill; 🚌104, 113, 124)

Old Calton Burial Ground CEMETERY

9 ◉ MAP P100, G4

One of Edinburgh's many atmospheric old cemeteries, Old Calton is dominated by the tall black obelisk of the **Political Martyrs' Monument**, which commemorates those who suffered in the fight for electoral reform in the 1790s. In the southern corner is the massive cylindrical grey stone **tomb of David Hume** (1711–76), Scotland's most famous philosopher.

Hume was a noted atheist, prompting rumours that he had made a Faustian pact with the devil; after his death his friends held a vigil at the tomb for eight nights, burning candles and firing pistols into the darkness lest evil spirits come to bear away his soul. (Waterloo Pl; 🚌15)

St Andrew Square SQUARE

10 ◉ MAP P100, E4

Though not as architecturally distinguished as its sister Charlotte Sq (p102), at the opposite end of George St, St Andrew Sq is dominated by the fluted column of the **Melville Monument** (St Andrew Sq; 🚇St Andrew Sq), which commemorates Henry Dundas, 1st Viscount Melville (1742–1811). Popular restaurants line the south side, while the east side is dominated by 2018's **Edinburgh Grand** luxury-apartments development. On summer afternoons the garden in the middle fills with lunching office workers who sip coffee from the square's espresso bar. (🚇St Andrew Sq)

Dundas House HISTORIC BUILDING

11 ◉ MAP P100, E4

The impressive Palladian mansion of Dundas House, built between 1772 and 1774 on the eastern side of St Andrew Sq, was built for Sir Laurence Dundas (1712–81). It has been the head office of the Royal Bank of Scotland since 1825 and has a spectacular domed banking hall dating from 1857 (you can nip inside for a look). (St Andrew Sq, EH2 2YB; 🚇St Andrew Sq)

General Register House
HISTORIC BUILDING

12 ◎ MAP P100, F4

The beautiful General Register House, designed by Robert Adam in 1788 and with a statue of the Duke of Wellington on horseback in front, houses the National Archives of Scotland and the **Scotlands-People genealogical research centre**. (☎0131-314 4300; www.scotlandspeople.gov.uk; 2 Princes St; ⏱9am-4.30pm Mon-Fri; 🚌all Princes St buses)

St Andrew's House
HISTORIC BUILDING

13 ◎ MAP P100, G4

On the southern side of Calton Hill stands the art deco facade of St Andrew's House, built between 1936 and 1939 and housing the civil servants of the Westminster government's Scottish Office until they were moved to the new Scottish Executive building in Leith in 1996. (Regent Rd; 🚌15, 18)

Eating

Outlook
SCOTTISH £££

14 ✖ MAP P100, G4

This glass-walled restaurant perched on top of Calton Hill enjoys some of the finest views in the city, and some of the finest food. Run by the same folk as Gardener's Cottage (p106), it has a menu consisting of a tray of seven small dishes (including a vegetarian option) prepared using whatever

Edinburgh Zoo

Opened in 1913, **Edinburgh Zoo** (Map p100; ☎0131-334 9171; www.edinburghzoo.org.uk; 134 Corstorphine Rd, EH12 6TS; adult/child £19.95/11.35; ⏱10am-6pm Apr-Sep, to 5pm Oct & Mar, to 4pm Nov-Feb; 👪; 🚌12, 18, 26, 31, 100) is one of the world's leading conservation zoos. Edinburgh's captive breeding programme has helped save many endangered species, including Siberian tigers, pygmy hippos and red pandas. The main attractions are the two **giant pandas**, Tian Tian and Yang Guang, who arrived in December 2011, and the **penguin parade** (the zoo's penguins go for a walk every day at 2.15pm). The zoo is 2.5 miles west of the city centre.

fresh local produce is in season, plus a choice of sides and wines. (☎0131-322 1246; www.thelookoutedinburgh.co; Calton Hill, EH7 5AA; lunch/dinner from £28/34; ⏱noon-9.30pm Tue-Thu, 10am-9.30pm Fri-Sun; 🍴)

Baba
MEZZE £

15 ✖ MAP P100, A5

Located on Edinburgh's premier George St and connected to the chic Kimpton Charlotte Square hotel, Baba specialises in uber-hip and sophisticated Levantine cuisine. The menu is short but exquisite, featuring stunning meze

New Town History

Between the end of the 14th century and the start of the 18th, the population of Edinburgh – still confined within the walls of the Old Town – increased from 2000 to 50,000. The tottering tenements were unsafe and occasionally collapsed, fire was an ever-present danger and the overcrowding and squalor became unbearable. There was no sewer system and household waste was disposed of by flinging it from the window into the street with a euphemistic shout of 'Gardyloo!' (from the French 'gardez l'eau' – beware of the water). Passers-by replied with 'Haud yer haun'!' (Hold your hand) but were often too late. The stink that rose from the streets was ironically referred to as 'the floo'rs o' Edinburgh' (the flowers of Edinburgh).

So when the Act of Union in 1707 brought the prospect of long-term stability, the upper classes wanted healthier, more spacious living quarters, and in 1766 the Lord Provost of Edinburgh announced a competition to design an extension to the city. It was won by an unknown 23-year-old, James Craig, a self-taught architect whose elegant plan envisaged the New Town's main axis, George St, following the crest of a ridge to the north of the Old Town, with grand squares at each end. Building was restricted to just one side of Princes St and Queen St, so that the houses had views over the Firth of Forth to the north, and to the castle and Old Town to the south.

During the 18th and 19th centuries, the New Town continued to sprout squares, circuses, parks and terraces, with some of its finest neoclassical architecture designed by Robert Adam. Today it is one of the world's finest examples of a Georgian cityscape, and is part of a Unesco World Heritage Site.

(Beiruti burrata, anyone?), and flavour-packed plates delivered straight off the charcoal grill. Baba ganoush doesn't get more smoky, addictive or beautifully presented than this. (📞0131-527 4999; www. baba.restaurant; 130 George St, EH2 4JZ; mains £9-15; ⏱noon-3pm & 5-11pm Mon-Thu, noon-11pm Fri-Sun; 🖊🚼; 🚍all Princes St buses)

Gardener's Cottage SCOTTISH ££

16 MAP P100, H2

This country cottage in the heart of the city, bedecked with flowers and fairy lights, offers one of Edinburgh's most interesting dining experiences – two tiny rooms with communal tables made of salvaged timber, and a set menu based on fresh local produce (most of the vegetables and fruit are from its own organic garden). Bookings essential; brunch served at weekends. (📞0131-558 1221; www.thegardenerscottage.co; 1 Royal Tce Gdns, London Rd, EH7 5DX; 2-/3-course lunch £15/19, 6-course dinner £60; 🕙noon-2pm & 5-10pm Mon-Fri, 10am-2pm & 5-10pm Sat & Sun; 🚌all London Rd buses)

Dishoom
INDIAN ££

17 ✕ MAP P100, E4

This Edinburgh restaurant was the Dishoom minichain's first opening outside London. Inspired by the Irani cafes of Mumbai, it serves exquisite Indian street food in upmarket surroundings; the breakfasts, including the signature bacon nan, are legendary. Hugely popular – book well ahead, or be prepared to queue for a table. A vegan menu is available. (📞0131-202 6406; www.dishoom.com/edinburgh; 3a St Andrew Sq, EH2 2BD; mains £9-15; 🕙8am-10pm Mon-Fri, 9am-10pm Sat & Sun; 🛜🍴♿; 🚊St Andrew Sq)

Urban Angel
CAFE £

18 ✕ MAP P100, D4

A wholesome deli that puts the emphasis on fair-trade, organic and locally sourced produce, Urban Angel is also a delightfully informal cafe-bistro that serves all-day brunches (porridge with honey, pancakes, eggs Benedict), mix-and-match salads and a wide range of light, snacky meals. (📞0131-225 6215; www.urban-angel.co.uk; 121 Hanover St; mains £6-11; 🕙8am-5pm Mon-Fri, 9am-5pm Sat & Sun; 🍴♿; 🚌23, 27)

St Andrew's House (p105)

Paul Kitching 21212   FRENCH £££

19 ⊗ MAP P100, H3

A grand Georgian town house on the side of Calton Hill is the elegant setting for one of Edinburgh's Michelin-starred restaurants. Divine decor by Timorous Beasties and Ralph Lauren provides the backdrop to an exquisitely prepared five-course dinner (£85) that changes weekly and features fresh, seasonal delights. Vegetarian menu available. (☎ 0131-523 1030; www.21212restaurant.co.uk; 3 Royal Tce; 3-course lunch/dinner from £32/70; ⊙ noon-1.45pm & 7-9pm Tue-Sat; 🛜 🖊; 🖵 all London Rd buses)

Number One   SCOTTISH £££

20 ⊗ MAP P100, F5

This is the stylish and sophisticated chatelaine of Edinburgh's city-centre restaurants, with a Michelin star sparkling on her tiara. Contemporary art hangs on lacquered red walls and the food is top-notch modern Scottish (paired wines for the seven-course tasting menu costs an extra £75 per person) and the service is just on the right side of fawning. (☎ 0131-557 6727; www.roccofortehotels.com/hotels-and-resorts/the-balmoral-hotel/restaurants-and-bars/number-one; Balmoral Hotel, 1 Princes St; 7-course tasting menu £110; ⊙ 6.30-10pm Mon-Thu, 6-10pm Fri-Sun; 🛜; 🖵 all Princes St buses)

Dome   SCOTTISH ££

21 ⊗ MAP P100, D4

Housed in the magnificent neoclassical former headquarters of the Commercial Bank, with a lofty glass-domed ceiling, pillared arches and mosaic-tiled floor, the Grill Room at the Dome is one of the city's most impressive dining rooms. The menu is solidly modern Scottish, with great steaks and seafood, or try afternoon tea in the elegant Georgian Tea Room.

The One O'Clock Gun

On Princes St you can tell locals and visitors apart by their reaction to the sudden explosion that rips through the air each day at one o'clock. Locals check their watches, while visitors shy like startled ponies. It's the One O'Clock Gun, fired from Mills Mount Battery on the castle battlements at 1pm sharp every day except Sunday.

The gun's origins date from the mid-19th century, when the accurate setting of a ship's chronometer was essential for safe navigation. The city authorities installed a time signal on top of the Nelson Monument that was visible to ships anchored in the Firth of Forth. The gun was added as an audible signal that could be used when rain or mist obscured the visual signal. An interesting little exhibition in the Museum of Edinburgh (p58) details the gun's history and workings.

Reservations strongly recommended. (☎0131-624 8624; www.thedomeedinburgh.com; 14 George St; mains £16-23, 2-/3-course lunch £20/25; ⏰10am-10pm; 🅿🚻; 🚇St Andrew Sq)

Ivy on the Square BRITISH ££

22 MAP P100, E4

The first Scottish outpost of London's famous celebrity haunt, the Ivy in Covent Garden, this classy but informal brasserie serves up traditional British dishes, from eggs Benedict for brunch through afternoon tea to the Ivy's classic dishes of steak, egg and chips, or shepherd's pie (made with red wine sauce and topped with cheesey mashed potato). A vegan menu is availahle. (☎0131-526 4777; www.theivyedinburgh.com; 6 St Andrew Sq; mains £15-19; ⏰8am-midnight Mon-Sat, 9am-10.30pm Sun; 📶🅿; 🚇St Andrew Sq)

Contini ITALIAN ££

23 MAP P100, B5

A palatial Georgian banking hall enlivened by fuchsia-pink banners and lampshades is home to this lively, family-friendly Italian bar and restaurant, where the emphasis is on fresh, authentic ingredients (produce imported weekly from Milan; homemade bread and pasta) and the uncomplicated enjoyment of food. (☎0131-225 1550; www.contini.com/contini-george-street; 103 George St; mains £18-24; ⏰8am-10pm Mon-Fri, 10am-10.30pm Sat, 11am-8pm Sun; 📶🅿🚻; 🚇all Princes St buses)

Cafe St Honore FRENCH £££

24 MAP P100, C4

With candlelight glowing against old polished wood and reflected from antique mirrors, this intimate French restaurant is the ideal place for a romantic dinner. Service is discreet, the menu is sumptuous and the wine list is long. You can get a two-/three-course set menu for either lunch or dinner for £23/28. (☎0131-226 2211; www.cafesthonore.com; 34 Thistle St Lane NW, EH2 1EA; mains £16-28; ⏰noon-2pm & 6-10pm; 🚇Princes St)

Bon Vivant BISTRO ££

25 MAP P100, C4

A firm favourite with New Town foodies, this European bistro-style place offers superb value for this part of the city, with a range of tapas-style 'bites' as well as standard main courses, and a changing menu of seasonal, locally sourced dishes such as sea trout with radish, toasted black onion seeds and parsley sauce. (☎0131-225 3275; www.bonvivantedinburgh.co.uk; 55 Thistle St, EH2 1DY; mains £14-19; ⏰noon-10pm; 📶; 🚇23, 27, 42)

El Cartel MEXICAN ££

26 MAP P100, C4

Small, dark, and invariably packed, El Cartel brings authentic, vibrant Mexican street food to Edinburgh, delivered superfast with a banging soundtrack and a bucket of hot sauces on each table. The menu is so concise you could memorise it, and there are daily-changing frozen margaritas. No reservations – get there before 6.30pm or the wait can be long. (☏0131-226 7171; www.elcartelmexicana.co.uk; 64 Thistle St; tapas £6-9; ⊙noon-10pm Sun-Thu, to midnight Fri & Sat; ☐24, 29, 42)

Scottish Cafe & Restaurant

SCOTTISH ££

This appealing modern restaurant (see 1 ◎ Map p100, D5) has picture windows providing a view along Princes Street Gardens.Try traditional Scottish dishes such as Cullen skink (smoked-haddock soup) and leek-and-potato soup, or seasonal, sustainably sourced produce including smoked salmon and trout, free-range chicken and pork. (☏0131-225 1550; www.contini. com/scottish-cafe-and-restaurant; The Mound; mains £9-15; ⊙9am-5pm Mon-Wed, Fri & Sat, to 7pm Thu, 10am-5pm Sun; ⏾🛗; ☐Princes St)

Holy Cow

VEGAN £

27 ⊗ MAP P100, E3

This hard-to-find cafe is hidden in a New Town basement close to the bus station, but well worth seeking out for its vegan burgers (portobello mushroom, Vietnamese tofu or soya and kidney bean, with chunky fries), and fresh and zingy Mexican salads loaded with chilli, coriander and lime juice. (34 Elder St; mains £6-12; ⊙10am-10pm; 🖋)

Time 4 Thai

THAI ££

28 ⊗ MAP P100, B5

Stylish modern decor, smartly dressed staff and designer table-

Dome (p108)

JEFF WHITE/SHUTTERSTOCK ©

ware put this place a cut above your average Thai restaurant. The menu matches the elegance of the surroundings, with authentic recipes and intense flavours perfectly presented. The two-/three-course lunch for £17/19 is great value. (📞0131-225 8822; www.time4thai. co.uk; 45 N Castle St; mains £13-19; ⏰noon-2.30pm & 5-11pm Mon-Thu, noon-11.30pm Fri & Sat, 1-11pm Sun; 🚻; 🚌24, 29, 42)

Drinking

Café Royal Circle Bar PUB

29 🚇 MAP P100, F4

The Café Royal is perhaps *the* classic Edinburgh pub; its main claims to fame are its magnificent oval bar and its Doulton tile portraits of famous Victorian inventors. Sit at the bar or claim one of the cosy leather booths beneath the stained-glass windows, and choose from the seven real ales on tap. (📞0131-556 1884; www.caferoyaledinburgh.com; 17 W Register St; ⏰11am-11pm Mon-Wed, to midnight Thu, to 1am Fri & Sat, to 10pm Sun; 📶; 🚌Princes St)

Lucky Liquor Co COCKTAIL BAR

30 🚇 MAP P100, C4

This tiny, black-and-white bar is all about the number 13: 13 bottles of base spirit are used to create a daily menu of 13 cocktails. The result is a playful list with some unusual flavours, such as tonka-bean liqueur, coconut champagne and

Bohemian Broughton

The lively, bohemian district of Broughton, centred on Broughton St at the northeastern corner of the New Town, is the focus of Edinburgh's gay scene and home to many good bars, cafes and restaurants. **CC Blooms** (Map p100, G3; 📞0131-556 9331; www.ccblooms.co.uk; 23 Greenside Pl; ⏰11am-3am; 📶; 🚌all Leith Walk buses), opposite the top end of Broughton St, is the city's biggest gay club.

salted grapefruit soda (though not necessarily all in the same glass!), served by a fun and friendly crew. (📞0131-226 3976; www.luckyliquorco. com; 39a Queen St, EH2 3NH; ⏰4pm-1am; 🚌24, 29, 42)

Joseph Pearce's PUB

31 🚇 MAP P100, H2

This traditional Victorian pub has been remodelled and given a new lease of life by the Swedish owners. It's a real hub of the local community, with good food (very family friendly before 5pm), a relaxed atmosphere, and events like Monday-night Scrabble games and August crayfish parties. (📞0131-556 4140; www.bodabar.com/joseph-pearces; 23 Elm Row; ⏰11am-midnight Sun-Thu, to 1am Fri & Sat; 📶🚻; 🚌all Leith Walk buses)

Guildford Arms PUB

32 ⊕ MAP P100, F4

Located in a side alley off the east end of Princes St, the Guildford is a classic Victorian pub full of polished mahogany, gleaming brass and ornate cornices. The range of real ales is excellent – try to get a table in the unusual upstairs gallery, with a view over the sea of drinkers below. (☏0131-556 4312; www.guildfordarms. com; 1 W Register St; ⏱11am-11pm Mon-Thu, to 11.30pm Fri & Sat, 12.30-11pm Sun; 🛜; 🚊St Andrew Sq)

Bramble COCKTAIL BAR

33 ⊕ MAP P100, D4

One of those places that easily earns the sobriquet 'best-kept secret', Bramble is an unmarked cellar bar (there's only an inconspicuous brass nameplate beneath a dry-cleaner's shop) where a maze of stone and brick hideaways conceals what is arguably the city's best cocktail venue. No beer taps, just expertly mixed drinks. (☏0131-226 6343; www.bramblebar.co.uk; 16a Queen St; ⏱4pm-1am; 🚊23, 27)

Abbotsford PUB

34 ⊕ MAP P100, D4

One of the few pubs in Rose St that has retained its Edwardian splendour, the Abbotsford has long been a hang-out for writers, actors and media people, and has many loyal regulars. Named after Sir Walter Scott's country house, it dates from 1902; the pub's centrepiece is a splendid mahogany island bar.

There's a good selection of real ales. (☏0131-225 5276; www.theabbotsford. com; 3 Rose St; ⏱11am-11pm Mon-Thu, to midnight Fri & Sat, 12.30-11pm Sun; 🛜; 🚊all Princes St buses)

Clark's Bar PUB

35 ⊕ MAP P100, C2

A century old and still going strong, Clark's caters to a clientele of real-ale aficionados, football fans (there are three TVs), local office workers and loyal regulars, who appreciate an old-fashioned, no-frills pub with lots of wood panelling and polished brass, and cosy little back rooms for convivial storytelling. (☏0131-556 1067; www.facebook.com/ClarksBar Edinburgh; 142 Dundas St; ⏱noon-11.30pm Sun-Thu, to 12.30am Fri & Sat; 🛜🐾; 🚊23, 27)

Oxford Bar PUB

36 ⊕ MAP P100, B5

The Oxford is that rarest of things: a real pub for real people, with no 'theme', no frills and no pretensions. 'The Ox' has been immortalised by Ian Rankin, author of the Inspector Rebus novels, whose fictional detective is a regular here (as is the author himself). There's occasional live folk music. (☏0131-539 7119; 8 Young St; ⏱noon-midnight Mon-Thu, 11am-1am Fri & Sat, 12.30-11pm Sun; 🛜; 🚊all Princes St buses)

Cumberland Bar PUB

37 ⊕ MAP P100, D2

Immortalised as the stereotypical New Town pub in Alexander McCall

Smith's serialised novel *44 Scotland Street,* the Cumberland has an authentic, traditional wood-brass-and-mirrors look (despite being relatively new) and serves well-looked-after, cask-conditioned ales and a wide range of malt whiskies. There's also a pleasant little beer garden. (☑ 0131-558 3134; www.cumberlandbar.co.uk; 1-3 Cumberland St; ☉ noon-midnight Mon-Wed, to 1am Thu-Sat, 11am-11pm Sun; 🛜; 🚌 23, 27)

Tigerlily   COCKTAIL BAR

38 ⭐ MAP P100, B5

The swirling textured wallpapers, glittering mirror-mosaic pillars, modernist lighting and plush velvet armchairs have won a cluster of design awards for this boutique-hotel bar, where sharp suits and stiletto heels line the banquettes. There's a huge list of expertly mixed cocktails, plus a range of Scottish craft beers on tap. (☑ 0131-225 5005; www.tigerlilyedinburgh.co.uk/edinburgh-bar; 125 George St; ☉ 11am-1am; 🛜; 🚌 all Princes St buses)

Cask & Barrel   PUB

39 ⭐ MAP P100, F2

At the foot of Broughton St, the spit-and-sawdust-style Cask & Barrel is a beer-drinker's delight, with a selection of up to 10 real ales, as well as Czech and German beers, and an array of TV screens for keeping up with the football or rugby. (☑ 0131-556 3132; www.facebook.com/CaskandBarrelBroughtonStreet; 115 Broughton St; ☉ 11am-midnight Sun-Thu, to 1am Fri & Sat; 🚌 8, 23, 27)

Entertainment

Stand Comedy Club   COMEDY

40 ⭐ MAP P100, E3

The Stand, founded in 1995, is Edinburgh's main independent comedy venue. It's an intimate cabaret bar with performances every night and a free Sunday lunchtime show. (☑ 0131-558 7272; www.thestand.co.uk; 5 York Pl; tickets £3-18; ☉ from 7.30pm Mon-Sat, from 12.30pm Sun; 🚌 St Andrew Sq)

Voodoo Rooms   LIVE MUSIC

41 ⭐ MAP P100, E4

Decadent decor of black leather, ornate plasterwork and gilt detailing creates a stylish setting for this complex of bars and performance spaces above the Café Royal (p111), hosting everything from classic soul and Motown to blues nights, jam sessions and live local bands. (☑ 0131-556 7060; www.thevoodoorooms.com; 19a W Register St, EH2 2AA; free-£20; ☉ 4pm-1am Mon-Thu, noon-1am Fri-Sun; 🚌 St Andrew Sq)

Edinburgh Folk Club   LIVE MUSIC

42 ⭐ MAP P100, H3

The Ukrainian Community Centre is the home venue of the Edinburgh Folk Club, which runs a programme of visiting bands and singers at 8pm on Wednesday nights. (www.efc1973.com; Ukrainian Community Centre, 14 Royal Tce, EH7 5AB; £10; 🚌)

Literary Edinburgh

Sir Walter Scott

The writer most deeply associated with Edinburgh is undoubtedly Sir Walter Scott (1771–1832), Scotland's greatest and most prolific novelist, best remembered for classic tales such as *The Antiquary, The Heart of Midlothian, Ivanhoe, Redgauntlet* and *Castle Dangerous*. He lived at various New Town addresses before moving to his country house at Abbotsford.

Robert Louis Stevenson

Robert Louis Stevenson (1850–94) was born at 8 Howard Pl, in the New Town, into a family of famous lighthouse engineers. Stevenson is known and loved around the world for stories such as *Kidnapped, Catriona, Treasure Island, The Master of Ballantrae* and *The Strange Case of Dr Jekyll and Mr Hyde*, many of which have been made into successful films. The most popular and enduring is *Treasure Island* (1883), which has been translated into many different languages and has never been out of print.

Muriel Spark

No list of Edinburgh novelists would be complete without mention of Dame Muriel Spark (1918–2006), who was born in Edinburgh and educated at James Gillespie's High School for Girls, an experience that provided material for her best-known novel *The Prime of Miss Jean Brodie* (1961), a shrewd portrait of 1930s Edinburgh. Dame Muriel was a prolific writer; her 22nd novel, *The Finishing School*, was published in 2004 when she was 86.

Contemporary Writers

Walk into any bookshop in Edinburgh and you'll find a healthy 'Scottish Fiction' section, with recently published works by best-selling Edinburgh authors such as Candia McWilliam, Ian Rankin, Sara Sheridan, Alexander McCall Smith and Irvine Welsh.

Ian Rankin's Rebus novels are dark, engrossing mysteries that explore the darker side of Scotland's capital city, filled with sharp dialogue, telling detail and three-dimensional characters.

Although she was born in England, the publishing phenomenon that is JK Rowling famously began her career by penning the first Harry Potter adventure while nursing a coffee in various Edinburgh cafes; she still lives in Scotland.

Tigerlily (p113)

Shopping

Valvona & Crolla FOOD & DRINKS

43 🔒 MAP P100, G2

The acknowledged queen of Edinburgh delicatessens, established during the 1930s, Valvona & Crolla is packed with Mediterranean goodies, including an excellent choice of fine wines. It also has a good **cafe** (mains £7-14; ⊘9am-5.30pm Mon-Sat; 🛜🚻). (📞0131-556 6066; www.valvonacrolla.co.uk; 19 Elm Row; ⊘9am-6.30pm Mon-Sat; 🚌all Leith Walk buses)

Curiouser and Curiouser DESIGN

44 🔒 MAP P100, F2

A quirky independent boutique on hip Broughton St, selling everything from art prints to jewellery, homewares, stationery and books. The focus is on excellent design, with pieces by local and international artists, and prices that won't break the bank. Perfect for gifts and browsing. (📞0131-556 1866; www.curiouserandcuriouser.com; 93 Broughton St; ⊘11am-4pm; 🚌8)

Life Story HOMEWARES

45 🔒 MAP P100, E2

If you like your design stores grown up, Scandi inspired, and

Late Shopping Days

Most shops in Edinburgh open late on Thursday, till 7pm or 8pm. Many city-centre stores extend their late opening to all weekdays during the Edinburgh Festival in August, and during the three weeks before Christmas.

accompanied by coffee and cake served in elegant crockery, head to this shop, where you'll find quality homewares, accessories and jewellery. (📞0131-629 9699; www.lifestoryshop.com; 53 London St, EH3 6LX; ⏰10.30am-5pm Tue-Fri & Sun to 6pm Sat; 🚌8)

Scottish Gallery   ARTS & CRAFTS

46 🔒 MAP P100, C3

Home to Edinburgh's leading art dealers Aitken Dott, this private gallery exhibits and sells paintings by contemporary Scottish artists and the masters of the late-19th and early 20th centuries (including the Scottish Colourists). Appointments only on weekdays during the Covid-19 pandemic; walk-ins from 11am to 1pm Saturday. (📞0131-558 1200; www.scottish-gallery.co.uk; 16 Dundas St, EH3 6HZ; ⏰10am-6pm Mon-Fri, to 4pm Sat; 🚌23, 27)

Perre   JEWELLERY

47 🔒 MAP P100, B5

This tiny showroom specialises in handmade silver jewellery, offering a scintillating range of rings, bracelets, brooches and earrings in patterns to suit all tastes, including Celtic knots, thistles and naturalistic feather and leaf designs (📞0131-629 5515; www.perre.co.uk; 129 Rose St, EH2 3DT; ⏰11am-6pm; 🚋Princes St)

Alchemia   JEWELLERY

48 🔒 MAP P100, C4

Made in a workshop in St Andrews, Fife, the jewellery on display at Alchemia is designed in Scotland and inspired by the shapes and colours of the natural world. (📞0131-220 4795; www.alchemia.co.uk; 37 Thistle St, EH2 1DY; ⏰11am-5pm Tue-Thu & Sat; 🚌23, 27)

Palenque   JEWELLERY

49 🔒 MAP P100, C5

Palenque is a treasure trove of contemporary silver jewellery and handcrafted accessories made using ceramics, textiles and metalwork. (📞0131-225 7194; www.palenquejewellery.co.uk; 99 Rose St, EH2 3DT; ⏰10am-5pm Mon-Sat, 11.30am-4pm Sun; 🚋Princes St)

McNaughtan's Bookshop   BOOKS

50 🔒 MAP P100, G2

The maze of shelves at McNaughtan's basement bookshop – established in 1957 – houses a broad spectrum of general secondhand and antiquarian books, with good selections of Scottish, history, travel, art and architecture, and children's books. (📞0131-556 5897; www.mcnaughtansbookshop. com; 3a-4a Haddington Pl, EH7 4AH; 🕙11am-5pm Tue-Sat; 🚌all Leith Walk buses)

One World Shop   GIFTS & SOUVENIRS

51 🔒 MAP P100, A6

The One World Shop sells a wide range of handmade crafts from developing countries – including paper goods, rugs, textiles, jewellery, ceramics, accessories, food and drink – all from accredited fair-trade suppliers. (📞0131-229 4541; www.oneworldshop.co.uk; St John's Church, Lothian Rd, EH2 4BJ; 🕙10am-5.30pm Mon-Sat year-round, plus noon-5pm Sun Apr-Oct; 🚌all Princes St buses)

Harvey Nichols   DEPARTMENT STORE

52 🔒 MAP P100, E4

The jewel in the crown of Edinburgh's shopping scene has four floors of designer labels and eye-popping price tags. (📞0131-524 8388; www.harveynichols.com; 30-34 St Andrew Sq, EH2 2AD; 🕙10am-6pm Mon-Wed, to 8pm Thu, to 7pm Fri & Sat, 11am-6pm Sun; 🚇St Andrew Sq)

Jenners   DEPARTMENT STORE

53 🔒 MAP P100, E5

Founded in 1838, and acquired by House of Fraser in 2005, Jenners

is the 'Grand Old Lady' of Scottish department stores. It stocks a wide range of quality goods, both classic and contemporary.

Plans for Jenners to move to new premises in St James Quarter in 2021 have been put on hold because of the Covid-19 pandemic. (📞0131-225 2442; www.houseof fraser.co.uk; 48 Princes St, EH2 2YJ; 🕙9.30am-6.30pm Mon-Wed, to 8pm Thu, to 7pm Fri, 9am-7pm Sat, 11am-6pm Sun; 🚇Princes St)

John Lewis   DEPARTMENT STORE

54 🔒 MAP P100, F3

Remaining open while the new St James Quarter development (opening summer 2021) takes shape around it, this is the place to go for good-value clothing and household goods. (📞0131-556 9121; www.johnlewis.com; St James Quarter, Leith St, EH1 3SS; 🕙9am-6pm Mon-Wed & Fri, to 8pm Thu, to 6.30pm Sat, 10am-6pm Sun; 🚇York Pl)

Fopp   MUSIC

55 🔒 MAP P100, D4

A good place to hunt for cheap CDs and vinyl; the friendly staff really know what they're talking about. (📞0333 323 0670; www. fopp.com; 3-15 Rose St, EH2 2PR; 🕙9.30am-5.30pm Mon-Sat, 11am-5pm Sun; 🚌all Princes St buses)

Explore ◈

West End & Dean Village

Edinburgh's West End is an extension of the New Town, with Georgian terraces, garden squares and aupmarket shops along William and Stafford Sts. It takes in the Exchange district, the city's financial powerhouse, and Lothian Rd's theatre quarter, and in the west tumbles into the valley of the Water of Leith to meet picturesque Dean Village.

The Short List

○ **Scottish National Gallery of Modern Art (p120)** *Admiring 20th-century and contemporary art amid gorgeous landscaped grounds.*

○ **Dean Village (p123)** *Exploring this former mill village, a picturesque corner of central Edinburgh.*

○ **Theatre District (p129)** *Taking in a show around Lothian Rd at the Royal Lyceum Theatre, the Traverse Theatre, the Usher Hall or the Filmhouse.*

○ **Murrayfield Stadium (p130)** *Attending a rugby match at Murrayfield during the Six Nations tournament, a quintessential Edinburgh sporting experience.*

Getting There & Around

The West End is close to the city's only tram line, but you'll need a bus to get to the modern art galleries.

🚌 Lothian Buses 3, 4, 25, 33 and 44 head west from Princes St to the West End, going along Shandwick Pl to Haymarket. For Dean Village, take bus 13 from Hanover St, or buses 19, 36, 37, 41 or 47 from George St to Dean Bridge and walk down Bell's Brae.

🚌 Links the airport with the city centre, passing through the neighbourhood with stops at Haymarket and the West End.

Neighbourhood Map on p122

Dean Village (p123) PAMKA /SHUTTERSTOCK©

Top Sight 📷

Scottish National Gallery of Modern Art

Edinburgh's gallery of modern art is split between two impressive neoclassical buildings surrounded by landscaped grounds. As well as showcasing a stunning collection of paintings by the popular, post-impressionist Scottish Colourists, the gallery is the starting point for a walk along the Water of Leith.

◉ MAP P122, A2

☎ 0131-624 6200

www.nationalgalleries.org

75 Belford Rd, EH4 3DR

admission free

🕙 10am-5pm

🚌 13

Modern One

The main collection, known as **Modern One**, concentrates on 20th-century art, with various European movements represented by Matisse, Picasso, Kirchner, Magritte, Miró, Mondrian and Giacometti. American and English artists are also represented, but most space is given to Scottish painters – from the Scottish Colourists of the early 20th century to contemporary artists such as Peter Howson and Ken Currie.

Modern Two

Directly across Belford Rd from Modern One, another neoclassical mansion (formerly an orphanage) houses the gallery's annexe, **Modern Two**, which is home to a large collection of sculpture and graphic art created by Edinburgh-born artist Sir Eduardo Paolozzi. One of the 1st-floor rooms houses a recreation of Paolozzi's studio, while the rest of the building stages temporary modern-art exhibitions.

The Grounds

The gallery's collection extends to the surrounding grounds, featuring sculptures by Henry Moore, Rachel Whiteread, Julian Opie and Barbara Hepworth. There's also a sensuous 'landform artwork' by Charles Jencks, and the **Pig Rock Bothy**, a rustic timber performance and exhibition space created in 2014 as part of the **Bothy Project** (www.thebothyproject.org).

Antony Gormley's '6 Times'

A footpath and stairs at the galley's rear lead to the Water of Leith Walkway, which you can follow downstream for 4 miles to Leith. This takes you past **6 Times**, an Antony Gormley sculptural project of five human figures standing along the river (the sixth sprouts from the pavement at the gallery entrance).

★ **Top Tips**

o A free shuttle bus runs between the Scottish National Gallery and the National Portrait Gallery, with hourly departures from 11am to 4pm.

o On Saturday the gallery runs special tours and workshops designed for children; check the website (under Events) for details.

✕ **Take a Break**

Cafe Modern One (www.heritageportfolio.co.uk/cafes; 75 Belford Rd; mains £4-10; ⏱10am-4.30pm; 📶👶; 🚌13) has a terrace overlooking the sculptures in the grounds; **Paolozzi's Kitchen** (📞0131-332 5909; www.heritageportfolio.co.uk/cafes; 73 Belford Rd; mains £6-10; ⏱10am-4.30pm; 📶👶; 🚌13) in Modern Two is dominated by a huge metallic sculpture of Vulcan. Both serve cakes and coffee, plus hot lunch dishes from noon till 2.30pm.

West End & Dean Village

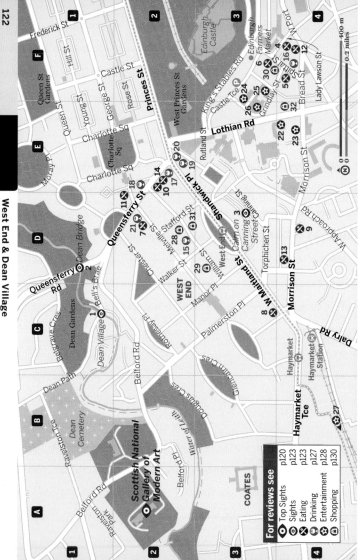

Frederick St

Hill St

Queen St Gardens

Queen St

Young St

George St

Rose St

Castle St

Princes St

West Princes St Gardens

Edinburgh Castle

Edinburgh Farmers' Market

N Port

Johnston Tce

Bread St

Lady Lawson St

King's Stables Rd

Castle Tce

Lothian Rd

Grindlay St

Morrison St

Charlotte Sq

Charlotte Sq

Moray Pl

Charlotte Sq

Queensferry St

Stafford St

Melville St

Chester St

Shandwick Pl

Rutland St

Canning St

Canning St

Festival Sq

Torphichen St

Manor Pl

Palmerston Pl

William St

West End

West Maitland St

Morrison St

WEST END

Glencairn Cres

Haymarket

Haymarket Station

Haymarket Tce

Dalry Rd

W Approach Rd

Queensferry Rd

Dean Bridge

Bell's Brae

Rothesay Pl

Dean Village

Dean Gardens

Belgrave Cres

Belford Rd

Dean Path

Ravelston Tce

Dean Cemetery

Water of Leith

Douglas Cres

Belford Pl

Belford Rd

COATES

Ravelston Park

Scottish National Gallery of Modern Art

0.2 miles

400 m

For reviews see	
Top Sights	p120
Sights	p123
Eating	p123
Drinking	p127
Entertainment	p128
Shopping	p130

Sights

Dean Village
AREA

1 ⊙ MAP P122, C1

Set in the valley that runs beneath the Dean Bridge ('dene' is a Scots word for valley), Dean Village was founded as a milling community by the canons of Holyrood Abbey in the 12th century, and by 1700 there were 11 water mills here, grinding grain for flour. One of the old mill buildings has been converted into flats, and the village is now an attractive residential area, with walkways along the river. (🚌 19, 36, 37, 41, 47)

Dean Bridge
BRIDGE

2 ⊙ MAP P122, D1

Designed by Thomas Telford and built between 1829 and 1832 to allow the New Town to expand to the northwest, the Dean Bridge vaults gracefully over the narrow, steep-sided valley of the Water of Leith. It soon became notorious as a suicide spot – it soars 27m above the river – and in 1912 the parapets were raised to deter jumpers. (🚌 19, 36, 37, 41, 47)

Calm on Canning Street
YOGA

3 ⊙ MAP P122, D3

This oasis of peace on a West End backstreet offers sessions of Vinyasa, Gentle Flow, Power and Yin yoga, including beginner classes. Book in advance online. (🕿 07704 472029; www.calmoncanningstreet. com; 16 Canning St, EH3 8EG; from £14;

🕐 7am-8pm Mon-Fri, 10.30-11.30am Sat, 4-6.30pm Sun; 🚋 West End)

Eating

Timberyard
SCOTTISH ££

4 ✕ MAP P122, F4

Ancient, worn floorboards, cast-iron pillars, exposed joists, and tables made from slabs of old mahogany create a rustic, retro atmosphere in this slow-food restaurant where the accent is on locally sourced produce from artisan growers and foragers. Typical dishes include honey-glazed monkfish with saffron, samphire and leek, and pigeon with radicchio, chanterelles and sherry. (🕿 0131-221 1222; www.timberyard. co; 10 Lady Lane St; mains £16-22, 5-course set menu £50; 🕐 noon-2pm & 5.30-9.30pm Tue-Sat; 🕿 ⚡ 🛉; 🚌 2, 300)

Kanpai Sushi
JAPANESE ££

5 ✕ MAP P122, F4

What is arguably Edinburgh's best sushi restaurant impresses with its minimalist interior, fresh, top-quality fish and elegantly presented dishes – the squid tempura comes in a delicate woven basket, while the sashimi combo is presented as a flower arrangement in an ice-filled stoneware bowl. Bookings recommended. (🕿 0131-228 1602; www.kanpaisushi.co.uk; 8-10 Grindlay St; mains £9-15, sushi per piece £4-10; 🕐 noon-2.30pm & 5-10.30pm Tue-Sat; 🚌 all Lothian Rd buses)

Water of Leith Walkway

The Water of Leith Walkway is a hidden thoroughfare linking the Scottish National Gallery of Modern Art to Stockbridge via Dean Village. It's a ribbon of green countryside in the middle of the city, and a haven for wildlife.

Terra Marique

ITALIAN ££

6 MAP P122, F3

It may say Italian restaurant on the front, but don't expect a pizza and pasta joint like the ones on nearby Lothian Rd – this is sophisticated, authentic Italian cuisine from a Sardinian chef, with a seasonal menu that includes the likes of monkfish roasted in lard with a casserole of black-eyed beans, and rabbit stew with polenta chips. (✆0131-229 0070; www.terra-marique.co.uk; 36 Castle Tce; mains £11-19; ⏱5-10pm Wed-Sun, noon-3pm Sat & Sun; ➔2, 35)

Westroom

ITALIAN ££

7 MAP P122, D2

Claiming to be Edinburgh's first cicchetti bar (Venetian cicchetti are like Italian tapas), Westroom serves up snack-size portions of nduja (spicy Italian sausage), meatballs, zucchini fries, white anchovies, and burrata (mozzarella cheese mixed with cream) with basil and tomato, as well as tempting antipasti platters of salami, prosciutto, pecorino, mozzarella and pickled vegetables. No under-18s. (✆0131-629 9868; www.thewestroom.co.uk; 3 Melville Pl; per portion £4-10; ⏱11.30am-10.30pm Tue-Sat; ➔13, 19, 36, 37, 41)

Omar Khayyam

INDIAN ££

8 MAP P122, C3

This is a modern Punjabi restaurant with attentive, waistcoated waiters, stylish modern decor and an unusual water feature trickling away in the middle of the dining room. The food is always fresh and flavourful, ranging from old favourites such as chicken tikka masala to more unusual dishes like Kabul chicken (with chickpeas, cumin and coriander). (✆0131-225 2481; www.omar-khayyam.co.uk; 1 Grosvenor St; mains £10-22; ⏱noon-2pm & 5pm-midnight Mon-Fri, noon-midnight Sat, 4.30pm-midnight Sun; ➔; Haymarket)

McKirdy's Steakhouse

SCOTTISH £££

9 MAP P122, D4

The McKirdy brothers – owners of a local butcher business established in 1895 – have cut out the middleman and now run one of Edinburgh's best steakhouses. The friendly staff here serve starters – such as haggis with Drambuie sauce – and juicy, perfectly cooked steaks, from rump to T-bone. (✆0131-229 6660; www.mckirdyssteakhouse.co.uk; 151 Morrison St; mains £14-32; ⏱5-10pm Sun-Thu, 5-10.30pm Fri & Sat; ➔2)

Vesta Bar & Kitchen

CAFE ££

10 MAP P122, E2

This appealing cafe-bar is made even more appealing by its partnership with Social Bite, a social enterprise set up to support the homeless (it also provides training and employment for homeless people). The food – from flatiron steak with poached eggs, to cauliflower-superfood tabbouleh – is delicious, and there are craft beers and creative cocktails to wash it down.

Cards on each table allow diners to 'pay forward' a small amount that goes to help provide free food for the homeless. (📞0131-220 0773; www.vestaedinburgh.co.uk; 7-8 Queensferry St; mains £10-18; ⏲noon-10pm Mon-Sat, 10am-5pm Sun; 🖳)

La P'tite Folie

FRENCH ££

11 MAP P122, D2

Housed in an unusual, Tudor-lookalike building, the upstairs dining room in this French-style bistro has a pleasantly clubbish feel, with candlelight, polished wood and leaded windows – try to grab the table in the little corner turret with its view of the spires of St Mary's Cathedral. Two-course lunches are £14.95. (📞0131-225 8678; www.laptitefolie.co.uk; 9 Randolph Pl; mains £14-25; ⏲noon-3pm & 6-10pm Mon-Thu, to 11pm Fri & Sat; 🛜👪; 🚌19, 36, 37, 41, 47)

Lovecrumbs

CAFE £

12  MAP P122, F4

Serving up Edinburgh's most creative and beautiful bakes,

Water of Leith

Lovecrumbs is a shabby-chic cafe popular with students and hipsters. Cakes and tarts are presented in a vintage dresser, and the artisan Steampunk coffee and the hot chocolate by Coco Chocolatier are second to none. Anyone for lemon-and-lavender cake with a rose-and-cardamom hot chocolate? (📞0131-629 0626; www.lovecrumbs.co.uk; 155 West Port; mains £3-6; ⏱9am-6pm Mon-Fri, 9.30am-6pm Sat, noon-6pm Sun; 📟2)

Cafe Milk
CAFE £

13 ✖ MAP P122, D4

This is fast food with a conscience – natural, nutritious, locally sourced and freshly prepared, from organic porridge to courgette, lemon and feta fritters, and North Indian dal with rice

or flatbread. Take away, or sit in and soak up the retro vibe amid old Formica tables and battered school benches. There are branches at Fruitmarket Gallery (p72) and Edinburgh Sculpture Workshop (p151). (📞0131-629 6022; www.cafemilk.co.uk; 232 Morrison St; mains £6-9; ⏱7.30am-4pm Mon-Fri, 8am-4pm Sat, 8am-3pm Sun; 🛜🖊; 🚇Haymarket)

Rendezvous
CHINESE ££

14 ✖ MAP P122, E2

Edinburgh's oldest Chinese restaurant, dating from 1956, is a no-frills, no-nonsense place, offering an extensive menu of Cantonese and Peking dishes, with classic favourites such as shredded beef with chilli sauce and aromatic crispy duck alongside more adventurous

Edinburgh Farmers Market

dishes including shredded sea blubber, boneless duck's feet with mustard sauce, and pickled cabbage with chilli sauce. (☎0131-225 2023; www.edinburghrendezvous.co.uk; 10a Queensferry St; mains £11-15; ☺noon-2.30pm & 5-10.30pm Tue-Thu, 5-11pm Fri & Sat, 1-10.30pm Sun; 🛜🖊♿; 🚌19, 36, 37, 47)

Drinking

Voyage of Buck
BAR

15 🚇 MAP P122, D2

You'll need to take a seat to peruse the 25-page drinks menu at this 'concept pub', themed around the exploits of a fictitious Victorian adventurer called Buck Clarence. Both the decor and the cocktails are inspired by the cities Buck visited on his supposed travels, including Paris, Cairo, Casablanca and Delhi – it's all tongue-in-cheek, a bit decadent, and great fun. (☎0131-225 5748; www.thevoyageofbuckedinburgh.co.uk; 29-31 William St; ☺10am-midnight Mon-Wed, to 1am Thu-Sun; 🛜🐾; 🚇West End)

Blue Blazer
PUB

16 🚇 MAP P122, F4

With its mosaic floors, polished gantry, cosy fireplace and efficient bar staff, the Blue Blazer is a down-to-earth antidote to the designer excess of modern bars, catering to a loyal clientele of real-ale enthusiasts, rum aficionados and Saturday horse-racing fans. (☎0131-229 5030; www.facebook.

Edinburgh Farmers Market
🍽⃝

This **market** (Map p122, F3; ☎0131-220 8580; www.facebook.com/EdinburghFarmersMarket; Castle Tce; ☺9am-2pm Sat; 🚌all Lothian Rd buses) is a colourful weekly event that attracts stallholders who sell everything from wild boar, venison and home-cured pedigree bacon to organic bread, free-range eggs, honey and handmade soap.

com/blueblazeredin; 2 Spittal St; ☺11am-1am Mon-Sat, 12.30pm-1am Sun; 🛜; 🚌2, 35)

Mathers Bar
PUB

17 🚇 MAP P122, E2

Established by wine merchant Hugh P Mather in 1902, this unapologetically old-fashioned pub retains many original features, including the decorative plaster ceiling and the massive mahogany gantry behind the bar (plus, some might argue, a few of the regular drinkers in front of it). With six real ales on tap, a friendly atmosphere and an open fireplace, it's a grand spot for a companionable pint. (☎0131-225 3549; 1 Queensferry St; 🚌19, 36, 37, 47)

Indigo Yard
BAR

18 🚇 MAP P122, E2

Set around an airy, stone-floored and glass-roofed courtyard,

Indigo Yard is a fashionable West End watering hole that has been patronised by the likes of Liam Gallagher, Pierce Brosnan and Kylie Minogue. Good food – including open-air barbecues during the summer months – just adds to the attraction. (☏0131-220 5603; www.indigoyardedinburgh.co.uk; 7 Charlotte Lane; ⊙8am-1am; 🛜👯; 🚌19, 36, 37, 41, 47)

Ghillie Dhu
PUB

19 🅘 MAP P122, E2

This spectacular bar, with its huge, chunky beer-hall tables, leather-sofa booths and polished black-and-white tile floor, makes a grand setting for the live folk-music sessions that normally take place here every night (from 10pm; admission free). (☏0131-222 9930; www.ghillie-dhu.co.uk; 2 Rutland Pl; ⊙11am-3am Mon-Fri, 10am-3am Sat & Sun; 🚌all Princes St buses)

Edinburgh Gin Distillery
DISTILLERY

20 🅘 MAP P122, E2

Gin aficionados flock to this urban distillery right in the heart of the city. Since starting out by making a classic, dry, London-style gin back in 2010, the Edinburgh brand has gone on to pioneer some creative flavour combinations, notably their delicious rhubarb and ginger gin. Tours include a tasting session (book ahead; no walk-ins until Covid-19 restrictions have been lifted). (☏0131-656 2810; www.edinburghgin.com; 1a Rutland Pl; ⊙10am-4.30pm; 🚌West End)

Cairngorm Coffee
COFFEE

21 🅘 MAP P122, D2

This light and bright Scandinavian-styled coffee shop is one of the most appealing places in town to linger over a flat white, complete with laptop friendly worktops and built-in iPads for free internet browsing. It does a great line in snacks too, including a mean pastrami sandwich with cheese, sauerkraut and pickles. (www.cairngormcoffee.com; 1 Melville Pl; ⊙9am-3pm; 🛜; 🚌)

Entertainment

Filmhouse
CINEMA

22 ✪ MAP P122, E4

The Filmhouse is the main venue for the annual **Edinburgh International Film Festival** (www.edfilmfest.org.uk; ⊙Jun) and screens a full programme of art-house, classic, foreign and second-run films, with lots of themes, retrospectives and 70mm screenings. It has wheelchair access to all three screens. (☏0131-228 2688; www.filmhousecinema.com; 88 Lothian Rd; tickets £7-11; 🛜; 🚌all Lothian Rd buses)

Henry's Cellar Bar
LIVE MUSIC

23 ✪ MAP P122, E4

One of Edinburgh's most eclectic live-music venues, Henry's has something going on most nights of the week, from rock and indie

FOTOKON/SHUTTERSTOCK ©

Ghillie Dhu

to 'Balkan-inspired folk', and from funk and hip-hop to hardcore, staging both local bands and acts from around the world. (☏0131-629 2992; www.facebook.com/Henrys cellarbar; 16 Morrison St; free-£10; ☺9pm-3am Sun & Tue-Thu, 8pm-3am Mon, 7pm-3am Fri & Sat; ☒all Lothian Rd buses)

Traverse Theatre   THEATRE

24 ⭐ MAP P122, F3

The Traverse is the main focus for new Scottish writing; it stages an adventurous programme of contemporary drama and dance. The box office is only open on Sunday (from 4pm) when there's a show on. (☏0131-228 1404; www.traverse. co.uk; 10 Cambridge St; ☺box office 10am-6pm Mon-Sat, to 7pm show nights; 🤳; ☒all Lothian Rd buses)

Royal Lyceum Theatre   THEATRE

25 ⭐ MAP P122, F3

A grand Victorian theatre located beside the Usher Hall, the Lyceum stages drama, concerts, musicals and ballet. (☏0131-248 4848; www. lyceum.org.uk; 30b Grindlay St, EH3 9AX; ☺box office 10am-5pm Mon-Sat, to 7pm show nights; ♿; ☒all Lothian Rd buses)

Usher Hall   CLASSICAL MUSIC

26 ⭐ MAP P122, E3

The architecturally impressive Usher Hall hosts concerts by the Royal Scottish National Orchestra (RSNO) and performances of popular music. (☏0131-228 1155; www.usherhall.co.uk; Lothian Rd; ☺box office 10am-5.30pm, to 8pm show nights; ☒all Lothian Rd buses)

Murrayfield Stadium STADIUM

27 MAP P122, B4

Murrayfield Stadium, about 1.5 miles west of the city centre, is the venue for international rugby matches. (www.scottishrugby.org; 112 Roseburn St, EH12 5PJ; Murrayfield Stadium)

Shopping

Gallery 10 ART

28 MAP P122, D2

This gallery specialises in modern and comtemporary art (exhibitions often include works by famous names including Picasso and Roy Lichtenstein) and promotes the work of both Scottish and international emerging artists, master printmakers and studio glassmakers. (www.galleryten.co.uk; 5 William St; 10.30am-5.30pm Tue-Sat; West End)

Lily Luna JEWELLERY

29 MAP P122, D3

If you're looking for a special present (or a special treat for yourself), look no further. This boutique stocks a glittering selection of earrings, necklaces, bracelets and brooches by independent designers including Anna Beck, Betsy Heilmann and Cristina Zani. Check out the Botanic Garden range by young Chinese jewellers inspired by traditional brush paintings and zen gardens. (0131-467 8245; www.lilyluna. co.uk; 43 William St; 10.30am-6pm Mon-Sat; West End)

Murrayfield Stadium

Assai Records

MUSIC

30 🔒 MAP P122, F3

An independent music shop that specialises in vinyl (old, new and remastered), Assai also has its own record label that promotes new Scottish talent. As well as a huge selection of discs, the shop stocks record players, band T-shirts and other music merchandise. (📞0131-228 3943; www.assai.co.uk; 1 Grindlay St, EH3 9AT; ⏰9.30am-6pm Mon & Wed-Sat, 10am-6pm Tue, noon-5pm Sun; 🚌2, 35)

Liam Ross

JEWELLERY

31 🔒 MAP P122, D2

Distinctive, hand-crafted jewellery is the hallmark of goldsmith Liam Ross. Choose from the range of gorgeous rings, bracelets and pendants on display, or commission a bespoke item from the man himself. Visit by appointment only during the Covid-19 pandemic. (📞0131-225 6599; www.jewellerybyliamross.com; 12 William St; ⏰9am-5.30pm Tue-Fri, 10am-5pm Sat; 🚌West End)

West End Shops

Edinburgh's West End has a string of high-street chain stores on the main drag of Shandwick Pl, but there's also a hidden enclave of independent designer shops along William St, between Manor Pl and Stafford St, plus the weekly food fest at the Edinburgh Farmers Market (p127).

Wonderland

TOYS

32 🔒 MAP P122, E4

Wonderland is a classic kids-with-their-noses-pressed-against-the-window toy shop that is filled with model aircraft, Lego *Star Wars* kits, radio-controlled cars and all sorts of other desirable things, but it also caters to the serious adult train-set and model-making fraternity. (📞0131-229 6428; www.wonderlandmodels.com; 97-101 Lothian Rd; ⏰9.30am-6pm Mon-Fri, 9am-6pm Sat; 🚌all Lothian Rd buses)

Explore ◈

Stockbridge

Stockbridge is a bohemian enclave to the north of the city centre, with an interesting selection of shops and a good choice of pubs and neighbourhood bistros. Originally a mill village, it was developed in the early 19th century on lands owned largely by painter Sir Henry Raeburn, who gave his name to its main street, Raeburn Pl.

The Short List

○ **Royal Botanic Garden (p134)** *Roaming the garden's 28 landscaped hectares, taking in the splendid Victorian palm houses.*

○ **Stockbridge Market (p143)** *Experiencing the neighbourhood's strong community spirit really coming alive on Sunday, when this market attracts the crowds.*

○ **Water of Leith Walkway (p140)** *Wandering along Edinburgh's river, the Water of Leith.*

○ **Scran & Scallie (p139)** *Enjoying the finest of Scottish food at TV chef Tom Kitchin's gastropub.*

○ **Shopping (p143)** *Browsing for gifts and souvenirs among the neighbourhood's many boutiques, galleries and independent shops.*

Getting There & Around

🚌 Lothian Buses 24, 29 and 42 run from Frederick St in the city centre to Raeburn Pl in Stockbridge. Bus 36 cuts across the neighbourhood from St Bernard's Cres and Leslie Pl to Hamilton Pl and Henderson Row.

Neighbourhood Map on p138

Circus Lane STEPHEN BRIDGER/SHUTTERSTOCK ©

Top Sight 📷
Royal Botanic Garden

Edinburgh's Royal Botanic Garden is the second-oldest institution of its kind in Britain (after Oxford's), and one of the most respected in the world. Founded near Holyrood in 1670 and moved to its present location in 1823, it has 28 beautifully landscaped hectares that include splendid Victorian glasshouses, colourful swathes of rhododendron and azalea, and a world-famous rock garden.

◎ MAP P138, C1

☏ 0131-248 2909

www.rbge.org.uk

Arboretum Pl

admission free

⊘ 10am-6pm Mar-Sep, to 5pm Feb & Oct, to 4µm Nov-Jan

🚌 8, 23, 27

John Hope Gateway

The garden's visitor centre is housed in this striking, environmentally friendly building overlooking the main Arboretum Pl entrance. There are exhibitions on biodiversity, climate change and sustainable development, as well as displays of rare plants from the institution's collection and a specially created biodiversity garden.

Glasshouses

A cluster of around 25 glasshouses in the garden's northern corner houses a huge collection of tropical plants. Pride of place goes to the ornate Victorian palm house, built in 1834 and home to vast rainforest palms, including a Bermudan palmetto that dates from 1822. The Front Range of 1960s designer glasshouses is famous for its tropical pond filled with giant Amazonian water lilies.

Rock Garden

Since it was first created in 1871, the rock garden has been one of the garden's most popular features. Boulders and scree slopes made from Scottish sandstone and conglomerate are home to more than 4000 species of alpine and subarctic plants from all over the world.

Sculptures

Pick up a map from the visitor centre so that you can track down the garden's numerous sculptures, ranging from a statue of Swedish botanist and taxonomist Carl Linnaeus (1707–78) by Scottish architect Robert Adam, to modern works by Yorkshire sculptor Barbara Hepworth and landscape artist Andy Goldsworthy.

★ Top Tips

o Guided walks around the gardens are at 11am and 2pm from April to October.

o The main entrance is the West Gate (Arboretum Pl), where the Majestic Tour bus drops off/picks up; city buses stop near the East Gate (Inverleith Row).

o Check the website for the current month's seasonal highlights.

✖ Take a Break

o The **Gateway Restaurant** (p137) in the John Hope Gateway visitor centre serves hot breakfast and lunch dishes.

o The **Terrace Cafe** (☎0131-552 0606; www.atthebotanics. co.uk; Royal Botanic Garden, Arboretum Pl; mains £5-8; ⏱10am-6pm Mar-Sep, to 5pm Feb & Oct, to 4pm Nov-Jan; 👶; 🚌8, 23, 27) has outdoor tables with a superb city-skyline view.

Walking Tour 🚶

A Sunday Stroll Around Stockbridge

Just a short walk downhill from the city centre, Stockbridge feels a world away with its peaceful backstreets, leafy Georgian gardens, quirky boutiques and art galleries, and the Water of Leith flowing through the middle. The strong community spirit comes alive on Sunday, when Stockbridge Market brings masses of local shoppers and browsers.

Walk Facts

Start Gateway Restaurant; bus: Royal Botanic Garden

Finish Stockbridge Market; bus: Kerr St

Length Two miles; 1½ hours

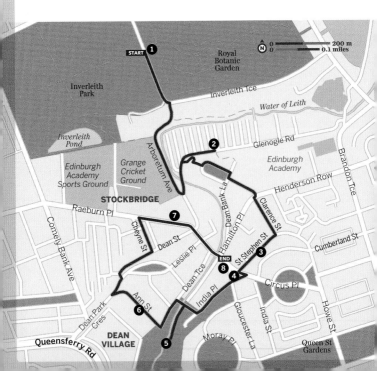

❶ Royal Botanic Garden

Take bus 8, 23 or 27 to its East Gate on Inverleith Row, and stroll through the park to the **Gateway Restaurant** (📞0131-552 2674; www.atthebotanics.co.uk; John Hope Gateway, Royal Botanic Garden, Arboretum Pl; mains £8-10; ⏱10am-6pm Mar-Sep, to 5pm Feb & Oct, to 4pm Nov-Jan; 🚌8, 23, 27) for breakfast with garden views. Choose from filled bagels, eggs Benedict, fruit salad or a full Scottish fry-up.

❷ Stockbridge Colonies

A short walk along Arboretum Pl and Arboretum Ave leads to the Stockbridge Colonies, a series of terraced stone houses built in the 19th century as affordable working-class accommodation (now not-so-affordable). Carved stone plaques on several gable ends show the tools of the tradesmen who built them.

❸ St Stephen Street

This side street is pure Stockbridge, crammed with galleries, boutiques, restaurants and basement bars. Miss Bizio (p144) has high-end vintage fashion, while Sheila Fleet (p144) showcases the work of the namesake jewellery designer. At St Stephen Pl is the Georgian archway that once led to the old Stockbridge meat market.

❹ Gloucester Lane

This steep, cobbled street was once the main thoroughfare connecting Stockbridge to the city, before the New Town was built. **Duncan's Land**, at the corner with India Pl – now Nok's Kitchen (p140) – is one of Stockbridge's oldest surviving buildings, dating from 1790.

❺ St Bernard's Well

A short walk along the Water of Leith Walkway leads to St Bernard's Well (p139), a circular temple built in 1789. The sulphurous spring was discovered by schoolboys in 1760, and became hugely popular during the late 18th century.

❻ Ann Street

The Georgian garden villas along Ann St (1817) are among the most beautiful and desirable houses in Edinburgh – the street is reckoned to be the most expensive in the city, and was named in 2008 as one of the UK's six most exclusive streets. It is also the setting for JM Barrie's 1902 novel *Quality Street*.

❼ Raeburn Place

Stockbridge's main drag is a bustle of shops, pubs and restaurants, with everything from chain stores and charity shops to craft shops, galleries and jewellery boutiques.

❽ Stockbridge Market

Sunday's Stockbridge Market (p143) is set in a leafy square, with stalls selling produce, soaps, cosmetics and more. Steampunk Coffee is located in a '70s VW campervan.

Stockbridge

For reviews see

◉ Top Sights	p134
◉ Sights	p139
✕ Eating	p139
◉ Drinking	p141
⌂ Shopping	p143

N 0 200 m
0 0.1 miles

Inverleith Park

Royal Botanic Garden

Inverleith Tce

Water of Leith

Inverleith Pond

Glenogle Rd

Edinburgh Academy Sports Ground

Grange Cricket Ground

Arboretum Ave

Henderson Row 25

Comely Bank Rd

13 Raeburn Pl
✕3
24 23 12
4✕

Dean Bank La
Hamilton Pl
Clarence St
St Stephen St

9

Dean St
Leslie Pl
Dean Tce
Kerr St
Deanhaugh St
Saunders St

18
19 14
22 7 16
17 20 10
2 21
6 8 15 5
NW Circus Pl

STOCKBRIDGE

Danube St
Ann St
India Pl
Doune Tce

Floatarium Spa

Dean Park Cres
Oxford Tce
Lennox St

St Bernard's Well
1

Gloucester La
India St
Jamaica St
11
Heriot Row

Queensferry Rd

Eton Tce
Water of Leith
Moray Pl

Dean Gardens

Sights

St Bernard's Well
MONUMENT

1 ◎ MAP P138, B6

St Bernard's Well is a circular temple with a statue of Hygeia, the goddess of health, built in 1789. The sulphurous spring within was discovered by schoolboys from George Heriot's School in 1760, and became hugely popular during the late-18th-century fad for 'taking the waters' – one visitor compared the taste to 'the washings of foul gun barrels'. It's open to the public on Doors Open Day (www.doorsopendays.org.uk) in September. (Water of Leith Walkway; admission free; 🚌 24, 29, 36, 42)

Floatarium Spa
SPA

2 ◎ MAP P138, C5

Escape from the bustle of the city centre in a warm, womb-like flotation tank, or enjoy the many other therapies on offer, including facials, aromatherapy massage, reflexology, shiatsu, reiki and Indian head massage (appointments necessary). There's a sweet-scented shop, too, where you can buy massage oils, incense, candles, homeopathic remedies and CDs. (📞 0131-225 3350; www.edinburghfloatarium.co.uk; 29 NW Circus Pl; 1hr treatment from £52; ⏱ 10am-3pm Mon, to 8pm Tue-Fri, to 6pm Sat, to 5pm Sun; 🚌 24, 29, 42)

Eating

Scran & Scallie
GASTROPUB ££

3 ✖ MAP P138, A4

Established by the Michelin-starred team responsible for Kitchin (p153), this laid-back gastropub adds a modern chef's touch to old-time dishes such as chicken-liver parfait, sausage and mash, and fish pie. There are also quality versions of classic pub grub such as burgers, steak pie, and fish and chips, as well as veggie options that include a spelt-and-lentil burger. (📞 0131-332 6281; www.scranandscallie.com; 1 Comely Bank Rd; mains £14-21; ⏱ noon-10pm Mon-Fri, 8.30am-10pm Sat & Sun; 📶 ♿ 🐾; 🚌 24, 29, 42)

Taisteal
INTERNATIONAL ££

4 ✖ MAP P138, B4

Taisteal is the Gaelic word for 'travel', so it's no surprise that the menu in this convivial bistro is a fusion of Scottish produce and flavours from around the world – pea and jalapeño soup with ham-hock croquette, and venison Wellington with butternut squash and blackberries are typical concoctions. There's also a five-/seven-course tasting menu for £40/50. (📞 0131-332 9977; www.taisteal.co.uk; 1-3 Raeburn Pl; 2-/3-course meal £25/30; ⏱ noon-2.30pm & 6-9.30pm Tue-Sat; 🚌 24, 29, 36, 42)

Water of Leith

Edinburgh's river is a modest stream, flowing only 20 miles from the northwestern slopes of the Pentland Hills to enter the Firth of Forth at Leith. It cuts a surprisingly rural swathe through the city, providing an important wildlife habitat (you can occasionally see otters and kingfishers) and offering the chance to stroll along wooded riverbanks only 500m from Princes St. The Water of Leith Walkway offers an almost uninterrupted 12-mile walking and cycling route along the river from Leith via Stockbridge and Dean Village to Balerno, on the southwestern edge of the city.

Pantry

CAFE £

5 ⚔ MAP P138, D5

The best breakfast spot in the neighbourhood, the Pantry serves no ordinary brunch. This is Stockbridge brunch, where the sausages are rare-breed pork, the black pudding comes from Stornoway, and the eggs are free range. There's even a soupçon of self-awareness – one of the most popular items on the menu is described as USA (ubiquitous smashed avocado). (www.thepantryedinburgh.co.uk; 1 NW Circus Pl; mains £8-12; ⏰9am-4pm; 📶👶; 🚌24, 29, 42)

Nok's Kitchen

THAI ££

6 ⚔ MAP P138, C5

Nok's dishes up a menu of authentic and beautifully presented Thai food in the romantic atmosphere of a 17th-century town house, decorated with Thai paintings, statues and woodcarvings. Two-course lunches are £10.95. (📞0131-225 4804; www.nokskitchen.co.uk; 8 Gloucester St, EH3 6EG; mains £11-19; ⏰noon-2.30pm & 5.30-10pm; 🚌24, 29, 42)

Bell's Diner

BURGERS £

7 ⚔ MAP P138, D4

It's doing the simple things well that counts, and Bell's has been doing pretty much the one thing – making burgers – *really* well since 1972. Whether your tastes run to classic beef patties or to lamb, chicken or veggie burgers, you're in for a treat. (📞0131-225 8116; www.bellsdineredinburgh.co.uk; 7 St Stephen St; mains £5-10; ⏰5-10.30pm Tue-Fri, 12.30-10.30pm Sat, 5-9pm Sun; 🍴👶; 🚌24, 29, 42)

Merienda

MEDITERRANEAN ££

8 ⚔ MAP P138, D5

Merienda (Spanish for 'snack') brings a tapas-style approach to its mixed menu of Mediterranean favourites (Serrano ham with Manchego cheese; lemon and coriander hummus) and seasonal Scots produce (smoked trout with Bloody Mary sorbet and cucumber; Scotch lamb kebab with tzatziki). There are tapas-size portions of pudding too (plum and bramble crumble with custard) and a tempting platter of Scottish cheeses. (☎0131-220 2020; www.eat-merienda.com; 30 NW Circus Pl; small plates £4-11; 🕑noon-2pm & 6-10pm Wed-Sun; 🚌24, 29, 42)

Pizza Express

PIZZA £

9 ✕ MAP P138, C4

Trust Stockbridge to have a designer pizza chain restaurant – housed in a former bank beneath a baronial clock tower, it has a stylish interior on two levels over-looking the Water of Leith, and a decked outdoor terrace right on the riverbank. The pizzas include such delights as the Veneziana

(onions, capers, olives, pine kernels, sultanas), plus a range of vegan pizzas. (☎0131-332 7229; www.pizzaexpress.com/edinburgh-deanhaugh-street; 1 Deanhaugh St; mains £8-12; 🕑11.30am-10pm; 🍴🚻; 🚌24, 29, 36, 42)

Drinking

Last Word Saloon

COCKTAIL BAR

10 🍷 MAP P138, D4

This cosy, dimly lit basement bar is unpretentious and just a little bit grungy. The cocktails are outstanding, with an extensive list including the complex Lear's Lyric (Hendrick's gin, ABA Pisco, manzanilla, avocado leaf, lemon, sugarsnap-pea syrup and celery bitters), and a small but interesting whisky menu – a good place

St Bernard's Well (p139)

PAMKA/SHUTTERSTOCK ©

to start exploring single malts. (📞 0131-225 9009; www.lastword saloon.com; 44 St Stephen St, EH3 5AL; ⏰ 4pm-1am; 🚌 24, 29, 42)

Kay's Bar

PUB

11 📍 MAP P138, D5

Housed in a former wine merchant's office, tiny Kay's is a snug haven with a coal fire and a fine range of real ales. Good food is served in the back room at lunchtime, but you'll have to book a table – it's a popular spot. (📞 0131-225 1858; www.kaysbar. co.uk; 39 Jamaica St, EH3 6HF; ⏰ 11am-midnight Mon-Thu, to 1am Fri & Sat, 12.30-11pm Sun; 🛜; 🚌 24, 29, 42)

Stockbridge Tap

PUB

12 📍 MAP P138, C4

This bar has more of a lounge atmosphere (with sofas at the back) than a traditional Edinburgh pub, but the counter reveals that it is dedicated to real ale – there are seven hand-pulled pints on offer, with three house and four guest beers. There's a good range of craft gins, too. (📞 0131-343 3000; www.facebook.com/thestockbridge tap; 2 Raeburn Pl; ⏰ noon-midnight Mon-Thu, to 1am Fri & Sat, 12.30pm-midnight Sun; 🛜 🍽; 🚌 24, 29, 36, 42)

Artisan Roast

COFFEE

13 📍 MAP P138, A3

Edinburgh's coffee scene punches above its weight, largely thanks to

Stockbridge Tap

Artisan Roast. The Stockbridge coffee shop is one of three branches in the city, plus there's a 'tasting lab' in Canonmills and their own roastery in Peffermill. This is coffee for serious coffee lovers, with a richly scented atmosphere of reverence. Great toasties too! (www. artisanroast.co.uk/stockbridge-cafe; 100a Raeburn Pl, EH4 1HH; ☺9.30am-4pm; ☎; ☑24, 29, 42)

Antiquary   PUB

14 🍺 MAP P138, D4

A dark, downstairs den of traditional beersmanship, with bare wooden floorboards and dark wood tables and chairs, the long-established Antiquary has lively folk-music sessions from 8.30pm on Thursday, and Wednesday quiz nights. (✆0131-225 2858; www. theantiquarybar.co.uk; 72-78 St Stephen St; ☺4-11pm Mon, 4pm-midnight Tue, noon-midnight Wed, noon-1am Thu-Sat, 12.30pm-midnight Sun; ☑24, 29, 42)

Bailie Bar   PUB

15 🍺 MAP P138, D5

Tucked in a basement, the Bailie is a Stockbridge stalwart – a dimly lit, warm and welcoming nook with a large circular island bar, a roaring fire in winter, and TVs screening live football. It serves good coffee as well as real ales and malt whiskies. (✆0131-225 4673; www.thebailiebar.com; 2 St Stephen St; ☺11am-midnight Mon-Thu, to 1am Fri & Sat, 12.30pm-midnight Sun; ☑24, 29, 42)

Shopping

Golden Hare Books   BOOKS

16 🔒 MAP P138, D4

Independent bookshops don't get lovelier than this. The Golden Hare – voted UK Independent Bookshop of the Year in 2019 – boasts a top-notch selection of books, an enchanting children's nook, and a small but perfectly formed events programme. A must if you love books, book design and beautiful shops. (✆0131-629 1396; www. goldenharebooks.com; 68 St Stephen St; ☺10am-6pm; ☑24, 29, 36, 42)

Stockbridge Market   MARKET

17 🔒 MAP P138, C4

On Sunday the local community's focus is Stockbridge Market, set in a leafy square next to the bridge that gives the district its name. Wares range from fresh Scottish produce to handmade ceramics, jewellery, soaps and cosmetics. Grab an espresso from Steampunk Coffee, which operates out of a 1970s VW campervan. (www. stockbridgemarket.com; cnr Kerr & Saunders Sts; ☺10am-5pm Sun; ☑24, 29, 36, 42)

Ginger & Pickles   BOOKS

18 🔒 MAP P138, D4

Not content with one independent bookshop, St Stephen St can boast another just across the road from Golden Hare, this one is devoted to children, all the way from parent-and-baby reading-together

Stockbridge Shops

Stockbridge is a good place to shop for gifts, crafts and jewellery. The main shopping areas are on Raeburn Pl, Henderson Row and St Stephen St, the last of which has a selection of boutiques selling everything from jewellery and vintage fashion to retro furniture.

books through to young adult fiction. (www.gingerandpicklesbook shop.com; 51 St Stephen St, EH3 5AH; 9.30am-6pm Tue & Fri, to 1pm Wed, to 7pm Thu, to 5pm Sat, 11am-4pm Sun; 24, 29, 36, 42)

Miss Bizio   VINTAGE

19 MAP P138, D4

Established by an enthusiast who has been collecting vintage fashion for more than 30 years, this boutique is a cornucopia of high-end clothes and accessories from the Victorian era to the 1970s. There's not much in the way of bargains, but it's fascinating to browse through. (07775 583675; www.facebook.com/missbizio; 41 St Stephen St; 11am-6pm Mon, Tue & Thu-Sat; 24, 29, 36, 42)

Sheila Fleet   JEWELLERY

20 MAP P138, D4

This Edinburgh gallery is a showcase for the work of Orkney-based designer Sheila Fleet, whose gold, silver and platinum jewellery is inspired by the colours and textures of her native islands' landscapes. (0131-225 5939; www.sheilafleet.com; 18 St Stephen St, EH3 5AL; 10am-5.30pm Mon-Sat; 24, 29, 36, 42)

Dick's   FASHION & ACCESSORIES

21 MAP P138, D5

Men's and women's fashion, accessories and homewares from small, independent manufacturers. (0131-226 6220; www.dicks-edinburgh.co.uk; 3 NW Circus Pl, EH3 6ST; 11am-6pm Mon-Sat, noon-5pm Sun; 24, 29, 42)

Ian Mellis   CHEESE

22 MAP P138, C4

The Stockbridge branch of the famous Old Town **cheese shop** (0131-226 6215; 30a Victoria St; 9.30am-7pm Mon-Sat, 11am-6pm Sun; 2, 23, 27, 41, 42), selling traditional Scottish cheeses, from creamy Hebridean Blue to sweet and nutty Loch Arthur cheddar. (0131-225 6566; www.mellischeese.co.uk; 6 Bakers Pl, Kerr St; 9am-7pm Mon-Fri, 8.30am-6pm Sat, 10am-5.30pm Sun; 24, 29, 42)

Annie Smith   JEWELLERY

23 MAP P138, B4

Annie Smith's back-of-the-shop studio creates beautiful and original contemporary jewellery in silver and 18-carat gold, with beaten and worked surfaces that reflect natural textures such as rock, ice and leaves. If there's

WILL SALTER/LONELY PLANET ©

Annie Smith

nothing in the shop that takes your fancy, you can commission Ms Smith to make something to order. (☏ 0131-332 5749; www.anniesmith.co.uk; 12 Raeburn Pl; ☉ 10am-5.30pm Mon-Sat, noon-5pm Sun; ☒ 24, 29, 42)

Galerie Mirages   JEWELLERY

24 🔒 MAP P138, B4

An Aladdin's cave packed with jewellery, textiles and handicrafts from all over the world, Mirages is best known for its silver, amber and gemstone jewellery in both culturally traditional and contemporary designs. (☏ 0131-315 2603; www.galeriemirages.com; 46a Raeburn Pl; ☉ 10am-5.30pm Mon-Sat, noon-4.30pm Sun; ☒ 24, 29, 42)

Adam Pottery   CERAMICS

25 🔒 MAP P138, D3

This small, independent pottery produces its own colourfully glazed ceramics, both decorative and functional, in a wide range of styles, with items ranging from coffee cups to garden planters. Visitors are welcome to visit the studio and watch the potters at work. (☏ 0131-557 3978; www.adampottery.co.uk; 76 Henderson Row; ☉ 11am-5pm Wed-Sat; ☒ 36)

Explore
Leith

Leith has been Edinburgh's seaport since the 14th century, but it fell into decay following WWII. It's now undergoing a steady revival, with old warehouses turned into luxury flats. There's also a lush crop of trendy bars and restaurants sprouting along the waterfront leading to Ocean Terminal, a huge shopping and leisure complex, and the former Royal Yacht Britannia.

The Short List

○ **Royal Yacht Britannia (p148)** Nosing around HM the Queen's former floating holiday home.

○ **The Shore (p151)** Strolling along the banks of the Water of Leith, trying to decide which restaurant to have lunch in.

○ **Pub Crawl (p155)** Sampling a pint of real ale in one – or several – of Leith's historic pubs.

○ **Kinloch Anderson (p158)** Choosing gifts at Edinburgh's finest kilt maker and tartan store.

○ **Leith Links (p151)** Visiting the place where the rules of golf were formalised in 1744.

Getting There & Around

🚌 Leith is well served by bus routes. Lothian Buses 16 and 22 run from Princes St down Leith Walk to the junction of Constitution and Great Junction Sts; from here, 16 goes west to Newhaven and 22 goes north to the Shore and Ocean Terminal; Bus 36 connects the West End to Leith via Stockbridge. Bus 200 links the airport to Ocean Terminal.

Neighbourhood Map on p150

Leith waterfront RICHIE CHAN/SHUTTERSTOCK ©

Top Sight 📷

Royal Yacht Britannia

Built on Clydeside, the former Royal Yacht Britannia was the British royal family's floating holiday home during their foreign travels from the time of her launch in 1953 until her decommissioning in 1997. The ship is now permanently moored in front of Ocean Terminal, and a tour provides an intriguing insight into the Queen's private tastes.

◎ MAP P150, B2

www.royalyachtbritannia.
co.uk

Ocean Terminal, EH6 6JJ

adult/child incl audio
guide £17/8.75

⊘ 9.30am-6pm Apr-Sep,
to 5.30pm Oct, 10am-5pm
Nov-Mar, last entry 1½hr
before closing

🚍 11, 22, 34, 36, 200

State Apartments

The *Britannia* is a monument to 1950s decor, and the accommodation reveals Her Majesty's preference for simple, unfussy surroundings. The Queen travelled with 45 members of the royal household, five tonnes of luggage and a Rolls-Royce squeezed into a garage on the deck. The **State Drawing Room**, which once hosted royal receptions, is furnished with chintz sofas and a baby grand piano Noël Coward once played.

Royal Bedrooms

The private cabins of the Queen and Prince Philip are surprisingly small and plain, with ordinary 3ft-wide single beds (the only double bed on board is in the honeymoon suite, used by Prince Charles and Princess Diana in 1981). The thermometer in the Queen's bathroom was used to ensure the water was the correct temperature.

On Deck

The Burmese teak decks were scrubbed daily, but all work near the royal accommodation was carried out in silence and had to be finished by 8am. When the ship was in harbour, one yachtie was charged with ensuring that the gangway's angle never exceeded 12 degrees. Note the mahogany windbreak added to the balcony deck in front of the bridge: it was put there to stop wayward breezes from blowing up skirts and revealing the royal undies.

Bloodhound

Britannia was joined in 2010 by the 1930s racing yacht *Bloodhound,* which was owned by the Queen in the 1960s. *Bloodhound* is moored alongside *Britannia* (except in July and August, when it's away cruising) as part of an exhibition about the royal family's love of all things nautical.

★ Top Tips

o You tour the ship at your own pace, using an audio guide. You'll need at least two hours to see everything.

o The Majestic Tour (p151) bus runs from Waverley Bridge to *Britannia* during the ship's opening times.

o The Royal Edinburgh Ticket (www. edinburghtour. com/product/royal-edinburgh-ticket) covers admission to *Britannia,* Edinburgh Castle and the Palace of Holyroodhouse, plus two days' travel on local tour buses.

✗ Take a Break

Britannia's sun deck (now enclosed in glass) makes a stunning setting for the **Royal Deck Tea Room** (www.royaly achtbritannia.co.uk; Ocean Terminal; mains £6-14; ⊙10am-4.30pm Apr-Oct, 10.30am-4pm Nov-Mar; ☺11, 22, 34, 36, 200), where you can enjoy coffee and cake, or even a bottle of champagne, with a view across the Firth of Forth to the hills of Fife.

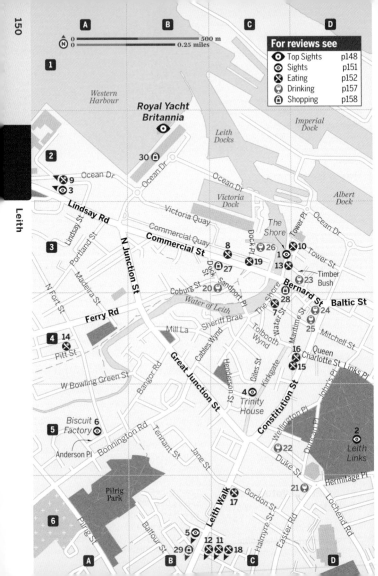

Leith

A B C D

N 0 ____ 500 m
   0 ____ 0.25 miles

For reviews see
◎ Top Sights	p148
◉ Sights	p151
✗ Eating	p152
◒ Drinking	p157
⌂ Shopping	p158

Western Harbour

Royal Yacht Britannia ◉

Leith Docks

Imperial Dock

30 ⌂ Ocean Dr

✗ 9
◉ 3
Ocean Dr

Lindsay Rd

Lindsay St

Portland St

N Junction St

Ocean Dr

Victoria Dock

Albert Dock

Victoria Quay

Commercial Quay

Commercial St

Dock Pl

The Shore

Tower Pl

Tower St

Ocean Dr

8 ◉ ⌂ 26 ✗ 10 1 ◉
19 ✗ 13 ✗

27 ⌂

Sandport Pl

Coburg St 20 ⌂

Bernard St

Timber Bush

23 ◒

Baltic St

Water of Leith

28 ◒

7 ✗ Maritime St

24 ⌂

25 ⌂

Mitchell St

Madeira St

N Fort St

Ferry Rd

Mill La

Sheriff Brae

Tolbooth Wynd

Cables Wynd

16 ✗ Queen Charlotte St Links Pl

15 ✗

14 ✗
Pitt St

W Bowling Green St

Bangor Rd

Great Junction St

Henderson St

Giles St

Kirkgate

Constitution St

4 ◉
Trinity House

John's Pl

2 ◉
Leith Links

Biscuit Factory 6 ◉

Anderson Pl

Bonnington Rd

Tennant St

Jane St

Wellington Pl

Duncan Pl

22 ◒

Duke St

Hermitage Pl

21 ◒

Lochend Rd

Pilrig Park

Pilrig St

Balfour St

Leith Walk

17 ✗ Gordon St

Halmyre St

Easter Rd

5 ◉
29 ⌂ 12 ✗ 11 ✗ 18 ✗

Sights

The Shore   AREA

1 ◉ MAP P150, C3

The most attractive part of Leith is this cobbled waterfront street alongside the Water of Leith, lined with pubs and restaurants. This was Leith's original wharf before the docks were built in the 19th century. An iron plaque in front of No 30 marks the King's Landing – the spot where George IV (the first reigning British monarch to visit Scotland since Charles II in 1650) stepped ashore in 1822. (🚌16, 22, 36)

Leith Links   PARK

2 ◉ MAP P150, D5

This public park was originally common grazing land but is more famous as the birthplace of modern golf. Although St Andrews has the oldest golf course in the world, it was at Leith Links in 1744 that the first official rules of the game were formulated by the Honourable Company of Edinburgh Golfers. A stone cairn near Duncan Pl on the western side of the park bears a plaque describing how the ancient game was played over five holes of around 400yd each. (🚌1, 21, 25, 42)

Edinburgh Sculpture Workshop   ARTS CENTRE

3 ◉ MAP P150, A2

This state-of-the-art building located on an old railway siding

The Majestic Tour

This hop-on, hop-off **tour** (www.edinburghtour.com/majestic-tour; St Andrew Sq; adult/child £16/free; ⏱daily year-round except 25 Dec) departs every 15 to 20 minutes from the north side of St Andrew Sq to the Royal Yacht *Britannia* at Ocean Terminal via the New Town, the Royal Botanic Garden and Newhaven, returning via Leith Walk, Holyrood and the Royal Mile.

is the first purpose-built centre dedicated to sculpture in the UK. There are regular exhibitions, talks and courses. Combine a visit with lunch at the top-notch on-site cafe run by Edinburgh's Milk and a stroll along the Hawthornvale path, which connects to the Water of Leith walkway. (📞0131-551 4490; www.edinburghsculpture.org; 21 Hawthornvale; admission free; ⏱9.30am-5pm Mon-Sat; 🅿; 🚌7, 11)

Trinity House   MUSEUM

4 ◉ MAP P150, C5

This neoclassical building dating from 1816 was the headquarters of the Incorporation of Masters and Mariners (founded in 1380), the nautical equivalent of a tradespeople's guild, and is a treasure house of old ship models, navigation instruments and nautical memorabilia relating to Leith's maritime history. Admission by prebooked guided tour only. (☎0131-554 3289; www.trinityhouseleith.org.uk; 99 Kirkgate; admission free; ⊙9.30am-4.30pm Mon-Fri; 🚌all Leith Walk buses)

Out of the Blue Drill Hall

ARTS CENTRE

5 MAP P150, B6

A multipurpose, family-friendly arts hub, Out of the Blue occupies a magnificent old drill hall dating back to 1901. It hosts events, exhibitions, classes, film clubs, a popular monthly flea market (p159) and ping-pong nights. It's also worth a visit for the cafe, which serves simple, home-style fare in arty, inclusive surroundings. (☎0131-555 7100; www.outoftheblue.org.uk; 36 Dalmeny St; ⊙10am-5pm Mon-Sat; 🚌all Leith Walk buses)

Biscuit Factory

ARTS CENTRE

6 ⊙ MAP P150, A5

This creative arts hub is housed in an old biscuit factory, also home to Edinburgh Gin's second distillery.

Events range from food markets to random club nights. Future plans include thye creation of 20 art and fashion studios over two floors, a cafe and bar, and a community garden on the roof. (☎0131-629 0809; www.facebook.com/biscuit factoryedin; 4-6 Anderson Pl; 🚌11, 36)

Eating

Restaurant Martin Wishart

FRENCH £££

7 ✗ MAP P150, C4

In 2001 this restaurant became the first in Edinburgh to win a Michelin star, and it's retained it ever since. The eponymous chef has worked with Albert Roux, Marco Pierre White and Nick Nairn, and brings a modern French approach to the best Scottish produce, from sautéed foie gras and langoustines with braised fennel to a six-course vegetarian tasting menu (£80). (☎0131-553 3557; www.restaurantmartinwishart.co.uk; 54 The Shore; 3-course lunch £39,

Seafood in Newhaven

Immediately to the west of Leith, Newhaven was once a distinctive fishing community whose fishwives tramped the streets of Edinburgh's New Town selling 'caller herrin' (fresh herring) from wicker creels on their backs. Sadly, modern development has dispelled the fishing-village atmosphere, with modern flats mixed in among the old cottages and terraces. The old fish-market building beside the little harbour now houses the **Fishmarket** restaurant, and the former church across the road is now home to an indoor climbing centre.

LEONID ANDRONOV/SHUTTERSTOCK ©

Newhaven harbour

4-course dinner £75; ⊗noon-1.30pm & 7-9pm Wed-Sat; 🍴; 🚌16, 22, 35, 36)

Kitchin

SCOTTISH £££

8 🍴 MAP P150, C3

Fresh, seasonal, locally sourced Scottish produce is the philosophy that's won a Michelin star for this elegant but unpretentious restaurant. The menu moves with the seasons, of course, so expect fresh salads in summer and game in winter, and shellfish dishes such as Orkney scallops baked in the shell with white wine, vermouth and herbs when there's an 'r' in the month. (🕿0131-555 1755; www.thekitchin.com; 78 Commercial Quay; 3-course lunch/dinner £39/90; ⊗noon-2.30pm & 6-10pm Tue-Sat; 🍴; 🚌16, 22, 35, 36)

Fishmarket

FISH & CHIPS ££

9 🍴 MAP P150, A2

As you might expect from the same team that runs Ondine, this harbourside place serves fish and chips that are a cut above the rest – not only haddock fresh from the Peterhead harbour, but also goujons of sole, monkfish in batter, grilled langoustines, even a whole lobster grilled with garlic butter (£30).

Or you can splash out on the seafood platter for two (£50), oysters and all. (🕿0131-552 8262; www.thefishmarketnewhaven.co.uk; 23A Pier Pl, Newhaven; mains £14-22; ⊗11am-10pm; 👶; 🚌11, 16, 200)

EDINBURGHCITYMOM/SHUTTERSTOCK ©

Restaurant Martin Wishart (p152)

Fishers Bistro

SEAFOOD ££

10 ✕ MAP P150, D3

This cosy little restaurant, tucked beneath a 17th-century signal tower, is one of the city's best seafood places. The menu ranges widely in price, from cheaper dishes such as classic fish cakes with lemon-and-chive mayonnaise to more expensive delights such as a whole Fife lobster with garlic-and-herb butter and chips (£45). (☎0131-554 5666; www.fishersbistros.co.uk; 1 The Shore; mains £12-26; ☉noon-10.30pm Mon-Sat, 12.30-10.30pm Sun; 🛜🚼♿; 🚌16, 22, 35, 36)

Little Chartroom

SCOTTISH £££

11 ✕ MAP P150, C6

A small restaurant with a big reputation, the Little Chartroom boasts just a few tables and four stools at the bar where you can watch the chefs constructing their complex, elegant dishes. The menu is equally small, with a choice of three starters, mains and desserts – typical offerings include roast monkfish with bacon, clams, hispi cabbages and girolle mushrooms. (☎0131-556 6600; www.thelittlechartroom.com; 30 Albert Pl; mains £20-30; ☉noon-2.15pm & 5.30-9.15pm Wed-Sat, 10am-1.30pm & 5.30-9.15pm Sun; 🚌all Leith Walk buses)

Twelve Triangles

BAKERY £

12 ✕ MAP P150, B6

Tucked away on an unassuming stretch just off Leith Walk, Twelve Triangles is an exceptional (and exceptionally tiny) bakery.

Some of the city's best artisan breads, pastries and coffee come out of its clever kitchen, and the doughnut fillings are legendary, encompassing pistachio custard, pink-grapefruit ricotta, and chocolate and peanut butter. Coffee and doughnuts don't get more sophisticated. (☎0131-629 4664; www.twelvetriangles.co.uk; 90 Brunswick St; mains £2-3; ⏱8.30am-2pm, or when sold out; 🚌all Leith Walk buses)

Shore
SEAFOOD ££

13 🍴 MAP P150, C3

The atmospheric dining room in the popular Shore pub is a haven of wood-panelled peace, with old photographs, nautical knick-knacks, fresh flowers and an open fire adding to the romantic theme. The menu changes regularly and specialises in fresh Scottish seafood, beef, lamb and game. (☎0131-553 5080; www.fishersrestaurants.co.uk; 3-4 The Shore;

mains £15-22; ⏱noon-10.30pm Mon-Sat, 12.30-10.30pm Sun; 📶👷; 🚌16, 22, 36)

Pitt
MARKET £

14 🍴 MAP P150, A4

A weekly street-food market surrounded by industrial warehouses, the Pitt is a little bit of East London in north Edinburgh. The regularly changing food trucks sell anything from buttermilk-fried chicken burgers to halloumi bao buns to haggis to sweet-potato pierogi (dumplings). Choose a drink from the wine and gin bars, or the Barneys beer truck selling local craft ales. (☎07534 157477; www.thepitt.co.uk; 125 Pitt St; entry £2; ⏱noon-8pm Sat, noon-6pm Sun Mar-Dec; 🚌7, 14, 21)

Chop House Leith
STEAK £££

15 🍴 MAP P150, D4

A modern take on the old-fashioned steakhouse, this 'bar and butchery'

Meals & Brews in Leith 🍽

Leith is renowned for its clutch of excellent restaurants, including two with Michelin stars – Martin Wishart (p152) and **Kitchin** (p153) – as well as lots of good-value bistros and pubs, many with outdoor seating and river views in summer.

With its long history as a dockyard neighbourhood, it's not surprising that Leith has more than its fair share of historic pubs, including Carriers Quarters (p158) and Port O'Leith (p158), plus newer ones housed in historic buildings, such as Teuchters Landing (p158). Plenty of modern bars, such as Nauticus (p157) and the Roseleaf (p157), have sprung up as well, catering to the inhabitants of newly developed apartment blocks and offices.

combines slick designer decor (the ceramic brick tiles are a nod to traditional butcher shops) with a meaty menu of the best Scottish beef, dry-aged for at least 35 days and chargrilled to perfection (chateaubriand for two goes for £80). Sauces include bone-marrow gravy and Argentine chimichurri. Cool cocktails, too. (📞0131-629 1919; www.chophousesteak.co.uk; 102 Constitution St; mains £17-30; ⏲noon-3pm & 5-10.30pm Mon-Fri, noon-10.30pm Sat & Sun; 📶; 🚌16, 22, 35, 36)

Hideout Cafe   CAFE £

16 ❌ MAP P150, D4

A snug retreat just a block away from Leith Links park (p151), the Hideout serves superb coffee (with some outstanding latte art) and a choice of breakfasts, from healthy granola with yoghurt and berries to more decadent smoked salmon and poached eggs on sourdough toast. (📞0131-555 5289; www.thehideoutcafe.co.uk; 40-42 Queen Charlotte St; mains £6-10; ⏲9.05am-5pm Mon-Sat, 10.05am-5pm Sun; 📶🐾; 🚌16, 22, 36)

Bross Bagels   BAGELS £

17 ❌ MAP P150, C6

Started up by a Canadian on a mission to bring authentic Montreal bagels to Edinburgh, Bross Bagels is the real deal. Dense, chewy bagels are made by a local Leith bakery, then stuffed with New York–style fillings such as pastrami with melted jack cheese and pickles, or turkey club with Montreal slaw and Mama Bross' rock sauce.

The original bagel shop is in Portobello, with a further branch in the West End (📞0131-629 4560; www.brossbagels.com; 105 Leith Walk; bagels £6-7; ⏲10am-3pm Mon-Fri, to 4pm Sat & Sun; 🥖🐾; 🚌all Leith Walk buses)

Stack Dim Sum Bar   CHINESE £

18 ❌ MAP P150, C6

This is the genuine article: a tiny, no-frills bar tucked off Leith Walk serving up the best dim sum in Edinburgh. The authentic menu includes silky-soft dumplings and rice rolls, the lightest char siu buns, and aromatic, crispy wontons. Seriously good food at seriously good prices. (📞0131-553 7330; 42 Dalmeny St; mains £5-9; ⏲noon-9.30pm Mon, Tue, Thu & Fri, noon-3pm & 6-9.30pm Sat & Sun; 🚌all Leith Walk buses)

Leith Farmers Market   MARKET £

19 ❌ MAP P150, C3

Taking over Dock Pl every Saturday, this small but bustling market is beloved by Leith locals, and sells everything from gourmet dog treats to fine Italian and French cheeses. Street food is provided by a rotating roster of traders. Make sure you check out the regulars: artisan coffee by the Bearded Barista and freshly baked croissants from Au Gourmand. (www.facebook.com/LeithMarketDockPlace; Dock Pl; ⏲10am-4pm Sat)

Walks in Cramond

Originally a mill village, Cramond has a historic 17th-century church and a 15th-century tower house, as well as some rather unimpressive Roman remains, but most people come to enjoy the walks along the river to the ruined mills and to stroll along the seafront. On the riverside, opposite the cottage on the far bank, is the Maltings, which hosts an interesting exhibition on Cramond's history. With its moored yachts, stately swans and whitewashed houses spilling down the hillside at the mouth of the River Almond, Cramond is the most picturesque corner of Edinburgh.

Drinking

Roseleaf   BAR

20 🚇 MAP P150, C3

Cute, quaint, and decked out in flowered wallpaper, old furniture and rose-patterned china (cocktails are served in teapots), the Roseleaf could hardly be further from the average Leith bar. The real ales and bottled beers are complemented by a range of speciality teas, coffees and fruit drinks (including rose lemonade), and well-above-average pub grub (served from 10am to 10pm). (📱0131-476 5268; www.roseleaf.co.uk; 23-24 Sandport Pl; ⏱10am-1am; 🛜♿; 🚌16, 22, 35, 36)

Nauticus   PUB

21 🚇 MAP P150, D6

Drawing on Leith's trading heritage with a retro maritime design and themed cocktails, Nauticus is a traditional community boozer gone hipster. The Victorian fixtures

and fittings may remain, but the artisan Scottish produce, extensive drinks list and live piano sessions make Nauticus a contender for coolest pub in Leith. Even the bar stools are upholstered with Harris tweed. (📱0131-629 9055; www.nauticusbar.co.uk; 142 Duke St; ⏱3pm-midnight Sun-Thu, to 1am Fri & Sat; 🚌1, 21, 25, 49)

Lioness of Leith   BAR

22 🚇 MAP P150, C5

Duke St was always one of the rougher corners of Leith, but the emergence of pubs like the Lioness is a sure sign of gentrification. Distressed timber and battered leather benches are surrounded by vintage objets trouvés, a pinball machine and a pop-art print of Allen Ginsberg. There are good beers and cocktails, and a tempting menu of gourmet burgers. (📱0131-629 0580; www.thelionessofleith.co.uk; 21-25 Duke St; ⏱noon-1am Mon-Thu, 11am-1am Fri-Sun; 🛜; 🚌21, 34, 35)

Carriers Quarters

PUB

23 🚇 MAP P150, D3

With a low wooden ceiling, stone walls and a fine old fireplace, the Carriers has all the historic atmosphere that its 18th-century origins would imply. It serves real ales and malt whiskies, as well as traditional Scottish bar meals such as pies, stovies (a meat and potato dish) and haggis. (☑0131-554 4122; www.facebook.com/CarriersQ; 42 Bernard St; ⏱noon-1am; 🐾; 🚌16, 22, 36)

Nobles

PUB

24 🚇 MAP P150, D4

In an area stuffed with choice pubs, Nobles might be the most loved by locals. This beautifully restored Victorian cafe-bar in the heart of Leith has original stained-glass windows, wood panelling and a nautical theme that speaks to the history of this old port. The food is straightforward and modestly priced and the choice of ales excellent. (☑0131-629 7215; http://new.noblesbarleith.co.uk; 44a Constitution St; ⏱10am-11pm Tue, Wed & Sun, to midnight Thu, to 1am Fri & Sat; 🚌16, 22, 36)

Port O'Leith

PUB

25 🚇 MAP P150, D4

This good old-fashioned local boozer has been sympathetically restored – it appeared in the 2013 film Sunshine on Leith. Its nautical history is evident in the form of flags and cap bands left behind by visiting sailors (Leith docks are just down the road). Pop in for a pint and you'll probably stay until closing time. (☑0131-554 3568; www.facebook.com/ThePortOLeith-Bar; 58 Constitution St; ⏱11am-1am Mon-Sat, noon-1am Sun; 🚌16, 22, 35, 36)

Teuchters Landing

PUB

26 🚇 MAP P150, C3

A cosy warren of timber-lined nooks and crannies housed in a single-storey red-brick building (once a waiting room for ferries across the Firth of Forth), this real-ale and malt-whisky bar also has tables on a floating terrace in the dock. (☑0131-554 7427; www.teuchtersbar.co.uk; 1c Dock Pl; ⏱10.30am-1am; 📶; 🚌16, 22, 35, 36)

Shopping

Kinloch Anderson

FASHION & ACCESSORIES

27 🔒 MAP P150, C3

One of the best tartan shops in Edinburgh, Kinloch Anderson was founded in 1868 and is still family run. It is a supplier of kilts and Highland dress to the royal family. (☑0131-555 1390; www.kinlochanderson.com; 4 Dock St; ⏱9am-5.30pm Mon-Sat; 🚌16, 22, 35, 36)

Flux

ARTS & CRAFTS

28 🔒 MAP P150, C3

Flux is an outlet for contemporary British and overseas arts and crafts, including stained glass,

EDINBURGHCITYMOM/SHUTTERSTOCK ©

Ocean Terminal

metalware, jewellery and ceramics, all ethically sourced and much of it made using recycled materials. (☏0131-554 4075; www.get2flux.co.uk; 55 Bernard St; ⊙10.30am-5pm Mon-Sat, 11am-4pm Sun; ⎙16, 22, 36)

Out of the Blue   MARKET

29 🔒 MAP P150, B6

A Paris-style flea market it ain't, but this monthly rummage through the back of Leith's collective cupboards is an interesting place to trawl for vintage clothes and accessories, old books, tools, toys and scratched vinyl. (www.edinburghfleamarket.blogspot.co.uk; Drill Hall, 36 Dalmeny St; ⊙10am-3pm last Sat of month; 📶♿; ⎙all Leith Walk buses)

Ocean Terminal   MALL

30 🔒 MAP P150, B2

Anchored by Debenhams department store, Ocean Terminal is home to fashion outlets including New Look, GAP, Schuh, Superdry and White Stuff. The complex also includes access to the former Royal Yacht *Britannia* and a berth for visiting cruise liners. (☏0131-555 8888; www.oceanterminal.com; Ocean Dr; ⊙10am-8pm Mon-Fri, to 7pm Sat, 11am-6pm Sun; 📶; ⎙11, 22, 34, 36, 200)

Explore ⊕

South Edinburgh

Stretching south from the Old Town and taking in the 19th-century tenements of Tollcross, Bruntsfield, Marchmont and Sciennes (pronounced 'sheens'), and the upmarket suburbs of Newington, Grange and Morningside, this is a peaceful residential neighbourhood of smart Victorian flats and spacious garden villas. There's not much by way of tourist attractions, but there are many good restaurants, cafes and pubs.

The Short List

○ **Surgeons' Hall Museums (p164)** Examining the gruesome but fascinating collection of medical specimens, surgical and dental instruments and historical curiosities.

○ **The Meadows (p165)** Relaxing in this lovely, tree-lined park to the south of the Old Town.

○ **Summerhall (p164)** Admiring the art at Edinburgh University's former veterinary school, now an arts and cultural centre.

○ **Blackford Hill (p166)** Taking in the view from this craggy hilltop.

○ **Bennet's Bar (p170)** Sampling the range of single-malt whiskies on offer at one of Edinburgh's classic Victorian pubs.

Getting There & Around

South Edinburgh covers a large area, and you'll need a bus to get to the farther-flung parts.

🚌 The main routes from the city centre are 10, 11, 15, 16, 23, 27 and 36 from Princes St to Tollcross, and 3, 5, 7, 8, 29, 31, 37, 47 and 49 from North Bridge to Newington.

Neighbourhood Map on p162

Victorian tenement housing in Morningside DRMAFILM/SHUTTERSTOCK ©

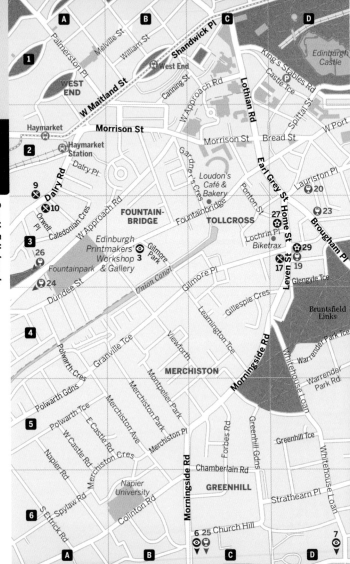

South Edinburgh

A **B** **C** **D**

1

Palmerston Pl
Melville St
William St
Shandwick Pl
West End
King's Stables Rd
Edinburgh
Castle
Castle Tce
Spittal St
WEST
END
W Maitland St
Canning St
W Approach Rd
Lothian Rd
W Port

2

Haymarket
Morrison St
Morrison St
Bread St
Haymarket
Station
Dalry Rd
Dalry Pl
Gardner's Cres
Earl Grey St
Home St
Lauriston Pl
20

3

9
10
Orwell Pl
Caledonian Cres
W Approach Rd
FOUNTAIN-
BRIDGE
Loudon's
Café &
Bakery
Ponton St
Fountainbridge
TOLLCROSS
27
Lochrin Pl
Biketrax
Leven St
23
29
17 19
Glengyle Tce

26
Edinburgh
Printmakers'
Workshop 3
& Gallery
Fountainpark
Gilmore Park
Gilmore Pl
Union Canal
Gilmore Pl
Gillespie Cres
Leamington Tce
Bruntsfield
Links
Warrender Park Rd
24
Dundee St

4

Polwarth Cres
Granville Tce
Viewforth
MERCHISTON
Morningside Rd
Warrender
Park Rd

5

Polwarth Gdns
Polwarth Tce
Merchiston Ave
E Castle Rd
Merchiston Cres
Montpelier Park
Merchiston Park
Merchiston Pl
Greenhill Gdns
Forbes Rd
Greenhill Tce
Whitehouse Loan

Napier Rd
W Castle Rd
Chamberlain Rd
GREENHILL
Greenhill
Strathearn Pl

6

S Ettrick Rd
Spylaw Rd
Napier
University
Colinton Rd
Morningside Rd
6 25 Church Hill
7

A **B** **C** **D**

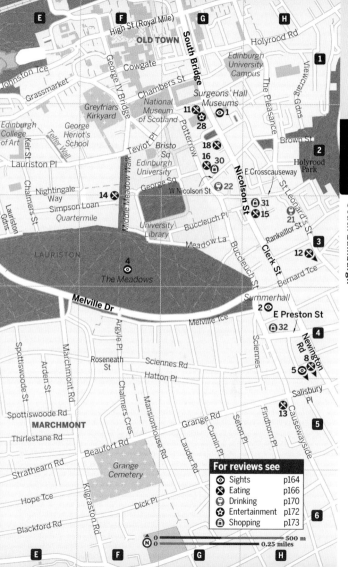

OLD TOWN

High St (Royal Mile)

South Bridge

Holyrood Rd

Edinburgh University Campus

The Pleasance

Viewcraig Gdns

Cowgate

Chambers St

Johnston Ice

Grassmarket

Greyfriars Kirkyard

George IV Bridge

National Museum of Scotland

Surgeons' Hall Museums

11 ⊗ ★
28

1 ⊙

Brown St

Edinburgh College of Art

George Heriot's School

Teller Wall

Edinburgh University

Teviot Pl

Bristo Sq

Potterrow

18 ⊗

Holyrood Park

St Leonard's St

Lauriston Pl

Chalmers St

Keir St

Nightingale Way

Simpson Loan

Quartermile

14 ⊗

Middle Meadow Walk

16 ⊗
30 ⋒

George Sq

W Nicolson St
? 22

E Crosscauseway

31 ⊙
15 ⊗

Nicolson St

Lauriston Gdns

University Library

Buccleuch Pl

Meadow La

Rankeillor St

21 ⋒

12 ⊗

LAURISTON

4 ⊙
The Meadows

Buccleuch St

Clerk St

Bernard Tce

Melville Dr

Argyle Pl

Melville Tce

Summerhall

2 ⊙
E Preston St

32 ⋒

Newington Rd

Roseneath St

Sciennes Rd

Hatton Pl

Sciennes

5 ⊙
8 ⊙ ▼

Salisbury Pl

Causewayside

MARCHMONT

Spottiswoode St

Arden St

Marchmont Rd

Chalmers Cres

Mansionhouse Rd

Grange Rd

Seton Pl

Cumin Pl

Lauder Rd

Findhorn Pl

13 ⊗

Spottiswoode Rd

Thirlestane Rd

Beaufort Rd

Strathearn Rd

Grange Cemetery

Kilgraston Rd

Hope Tce

Dick Pl

Blackford Rd

For reviews see

⊙ Sights	p164
⊗ Eating	p166
⊙ Drinking	p170
★ Entertainment	p172
⋒ Shopping	p173

0 ————— 500 m
0 ————— 0.25 miles

E F G H

Sights

Surgeons' Hall Museums

MUSEUM

1 ◉ MAP P162, G2

Housed in a grand Ionic temple designed by William Playfair in 1832, these three fascinating museums were originally established as teaching collections. The **History of Surgery Museum** provides a look at surgery in Scotland from the 15th century to the present day. Highlights include the exhibit on murderers Burke and Hare (p61), which includes Burke's death mask and a pocketbook made from his skin, and a display on Dr Joseph Bell, who was the inspiration for the character of Sherlock Holmes.

The adjacent **Dental Collection**, with its wince-inducing extraction tools, covers the history of dentistry, while the **Pathology Museum** houses a gruesome but compelling 19th-century collection of diseased organs and excised tumours pickled in formaldehyde. (☎0131-527 1711; www.museum.rcsed. ac.uk; Nicolson St; adult/child £8/4.50; ☉10am-5pm; 🚍all South Bridge buses)

Summerhall

GALLERY

2 ◉ MAP P162, H4

The Summerhall cultural centre houses several permanent art displays, and stages changing exhibitions of contemporary art. (☎0131-560 1580; www.summerhall. co.uk; 1 Summerhall; admission free; ☉11am-6pm Tue-Sun; 🚍41, 42)

Edinburgh Printmakers' Workshop & Gallery

GALLERY

3 ◉ MAP P162, B3

Founded in 1967, and now housed in a former rubber factory, this was the UK's first 'open access' printmaking studio, providing studio space and equipment for professional artists and beginners alike. You can watch printmakers at work in their studios, while two galleries hosts exhibitions of

Gilmerton Cove

While ghost tours of Edinburgh's underground vaults and haunted graveyards have become a mainstream attraction, **Gilmerton Cove** (Map p162; ☎07914 829177; www.gilmertoncove.co.uk; 16 Drum St, EH17 8QH; adult/child £7.50/4; ☉tours 11am-3pm Mon-Fri, noon-3pm Sat & Sun Apr-Sep, noon Mon-Fri, noon & 2pm Sat & Sun Oct-Mar; 🚍3, 7, 18, 29) remains an off-the-beaten-track gem. Hidden in the southern suburbs, the mysterious 'cove' is a series of subterranean caverns hacked out of the rock, their origin and function unknown. Advance bookings are essential (via the website).

The Meadows

lithographs and screen prints by local artists. There's also a shop and cafe. (📞0131-557 2479; www.edinburghprintmakers.co.uk; Castle Mills, 1 Dundee St, EH3 9FP; admission free; ⏰10am-6pm Tue-Sun; 🚌1, 34, 35, 300)

The Meadows PARK

4 ◉ MAP P162, F3

This mile-long stretch of lush grass criss-crossed with tree-lined walks was once a shallow lake known as the Borough Loch. Drained in the 1740s and converted into parkland, it's a great place for a picnic or a quiet stroll – in springtime its walks lie ankle-deep in drifts of pink cherry blossom, and there are great views of Arthur's Seat. (Melville Dr; 🚌all Tollcross, South Bridge buses)

Craigmillar Castle CASTLE

5 ◉ MAP P162, H4

If you want to explore a Scottish fortress away from the crowds that throng Edinburgh Castle, try Craigmillar. Dating from the 15th century, the tower house rises above two sets of machicolated curtain walls. The castle is 2.5 miles southeast of the city centre. From the bus stop on Old Dalkeith Rd walk 500m up Craigmillar Castle Rd.

Mary, Queen of Scots, took refuge here after the murder of her private secretary, David Rizzio; it was here, too, that plans to murder her husband Darnley were laid. Look for the prison cell complete with built-in sanitation, something some 'modern' British

The Pentland Hills

Rising on the southern edge of Edinburgh, the Pentland Hills stretch 16 miles southwest to near Carnwath in Lanarkshire. The hills rise to 579m at their highest point and offer excellent, not-too-strenuous walking with great views. There are several access points along the A702 road on the southern side of the hills. MacEwan's buses 100/101/102/103 run four to seven times daily along the A702 from Edinburgh Bus Station to Biggar.

prisons finally managed in 1996! (HES; www.historicenvironment.scot; Craigmillar Castle Rd; adult/child £6/3.60; ⏰9.30am-5.30pm Apr-Sep, 10am-4pm Sat-Wed Oct-Mar; 🚍24, 33, 38, 42, 49)

Hermitage of Braid
WILDLIFE RESERVE

6 ◉ MAP P162, C6

The Hermitage of Braid is a wooded valley criss-crossed with walking trails to the south of Blackford Hill – with sunlight filtering through the leaves and the sound of birdsong all around, you'll feel miles from the city. **Hermitage House** (Hermitage of Braid; ⏰9am-4pm Mon-Fri, noon-4pm Sun; 🚍5, 11, 15, 16), an 18th-century mansion, houses a visitor centre that explains the history and wildlife of the glen, and has details of nearby nature trails. (www.facebook.com/friendsofhermitage; 🚍5, 11, 15, 16)

Blackford Hill
VIEWPOINT

7 ◉ MAP P162, D6

A patch of countryside enclosed by the city's southern suburbs, craggy Blackford Hill (164m) offers pleasant walking and splendid views. The panorama to the north takes in Edinburgh Castle atop its rock, the bristling spine of the Old Town, the monuments on Calton Hill and the 'sleeping lion' of Arthur's Seat. (Charterhall Rd; 🚍24, 38, 41)

Eating

Condita
SCOTTISH £££

8 ✕ MAP P162, H4

The sheer quality of the food served in this intimate and sleekly stylish little restaurant, set in a converted Southside shop, made it Edinburgh's most sought-after table of 2019. A Michelin star followed in 2020; now you'll have to book as far in advance as you can to savour the seasonal, mostly organic delights that issue from its kitchen. (📞0131-667 5777; www.condita.co.uk; 15 Salisbury Pl; 8-course tasting menu £110; ⏰7-10pm Tue-Sat; 🚍all Newington buses)

Locanda de Gusti

ITALIAN **££**

9 ✗ MAP P162, A2

This bustling family bistro, loud with the buzz of conversation and the clink of glasses and cutlery, is no ordinary Italian but a little corner of Naples, complete with hearty Neapolitan home cooking by friendly head chef Rosario. The food ranges from light and tasty ravioli tossed with butter, sage and nutmeg to delicious platters of grilled seafood. (☎0131-346 8800; www.locandadegusti.com; 102 Dalry Rd; mains £14-28; ⏱5.30-10pm Mon-Wed, 12.30-2pm & 5.30-10pm Thu-Sat; 🚼; 🚌2, 3, 4, 25, 33, 44)

First Coast

SCOTTISH **££**

10 ✗ MAP P162, A3

This popular neighbourhood bistro has a striking main dining area with sea-blue wood panelling and stripped stonework, and a short and simple menu offering hearty comfort food such as maple-syrup- and mustard-glazed ham hock with spinach and nutmeg mash, or cod in banana leaf with lemon, basil, aubergine and shrimp paste. Lunchtime and early evening there's an excellent two-/three-course menu for £14.50/16. (☎0131-313 4404; www.first-coast.co.uk; 97-101 Dalry Rd; 2-/3-course dinner £22/26; ⏱noon-2pm & 5-11pm Mon-Sat; 🛜🌱🚼; 🚌2, 3, 4, 25, 33, 44)

Union Brew Lab

CAFE **£**

11 ✗ MAP P162, G2

Students with iPads lolling in armchairs, sipping carefully crafted espressos amid artfully distressed brick and plaster, recycled school-gym flooring, old workshop benches and lab stools... this is coffee-nerd heaven. There's good food, too, with hearty soups and crusty baguette sandwiches. In summer try the refreshing cold-brew coffee. (☎0131-662 8963; www.brewlabcoffee.co.uk; 6-8 S College St; mains £4-6; ⏱9am-5.30pm; 🛜; 🚌all South Bridge buses)

Edinburgh Food Studio

SCOTTISH **££**

12 ✗ MAP P162, H3

Far from the city-centre throng, Edinburgh Food Studio is a tiny unassuming restaurant and 'food research hub' dishing up some of the most creative, nerdy and – fear not – delicious cuisine in the capital. The bold, ever-changing menu ranges from a six-course tasting menu at lunch (£25) to a nine-course dinner, plus there are regular special events, tastings and guest chefs. (www.edinburgh foodstudio.com; 158 Dalkeith Rd; 9-course dinner £65; ⏱noon-2.30pm & 7.30-10.30pm Thu-Sun; 🚌2, 14, 30, 33)

No 1 The Grange

GASTROPUB **££**

13 ✗ MAP P162, H5

The menu at this friendly neighbourhood gastropub revolves

Brunch at Loudon's

One of South Edinburgh's favourite places to kick back over brunch with the weekend papers, **Loudon's** (Map p162, C3; www.loudons.co.uk; 94b Fountainbridge; mains £9-13; ⊘7.30am-5pm Mon-Fri, 8am-5pm Sat & Sun; 🛜🍴👶; 🚌1, 34, 35, 300) bakes its own organic bread on the premises, serves ethically sourced coffee, and has an all-day brunch menu (till 4pm) on Saturday and Sunday.

around a cluster of crowd-pleasing classics such as barbecue pork belly, fish and chips, gourmet burgers and even haggis, enlivened by daily specials like roast cod with fennel and broad beans. Brunch is served from 10am till noon at weekends, and includes waffles with bacon and maple syrup. (☑0131-667 2335; www.no1thegrange. co.uk; 1 Grange Rd; mains £13-20; ⊘10am-10.30pm; 🚌5, 42)

Söderberg (The Meadows) CAFE £

14 ✘ MAP P162, F3

This Swedish-style coffee house produces its own home-baked pastries and breads, which form the basis of lunchtime sandwiches with fillings such as roast beef with beetroot and caper salad,

and roast butternut squash with sunblush tomato pesto. Breakfast (served till noon) can be a basket of breads with conserves and cheeses, or yoghurt with granola and fruit. (☑0131-228 5876; www. soderberg.uk; 27 Simpson Loan; sandwiches £5-7, cakes £3; ⊘8.30am-5.30pm; 🍴👶; 🚌23, 27, 45, 47, 300)

Kalpna INDIAN £

15 ✘ MAP P162, H3

A long-standing Edinburgh favourite, Kalpna is one of the best Indian restaurants in the country, vegetarian or otherwise. The cuisine is mostly Gujarati, with a smattering of dishes from other parts of India. The all-you-can-eat lunch buffet (£9) is superb value. (☑0131-667 9890; www.kalpnarestaurant.com; 2-3 St Patrick Sq; mains £8-13; ⊘noon-2pm & 5.30-10.30pm; 🍴; 🚌all Newington buses)

Buffalo Grill STEAK ££

16 ✘ MAP P162, G2

The Buffalo Grill is cramped, noisy, fun and always busy, so book ahead. An American-style menu offers burgers, steaks and side orders of fries and onion rings, along with fish and chicken dishes, shrimp tempura and a handful of vegetarian options, but the steaks are the main event. (☑0131-667 7427; www.buffalogrill.co.uk; 12-14 Chapel St; mains £12-29; ⊘11am-9.30pm Tue-Sat, 5-9.30pm Sun; 🍴; 🚌41, 42)

Tuk Tuk

INDIAN £

17  MAP P162, D3

One of Edinburgh's livelier Indian restaurants, Tuk Tuk serves street-food-style Indian dishes in spacious surroundings with vintage Bollywood posters on the wall. The menu boasts classics such as *channa puri* (curried chickpeas with flatbread) and an excellent signature 'railway station' curry (lamb on the bone, as served on Indian railways). Popular with bigger groups and pre- and post-theatre crowds. (☎0131-228 3322; www.tuk-tukonline.com; 1 Leven St; mains £5-7; ☉noon-10.30pm Sun-Thu, to 10.45pm Fri & Sat; ☐11, 15, 16, 23, 36, 45)

Mosque Kitchen

INDIAN £

18 MAP P162, G2

Expect shared tables and disposable plates, but this is the place to go for cheap, authentic and delicious homemade curries, kebabs, pakoras and nan bread, all washed down with lassi or mango juice. It caters to Edinburgh's Central Mosque but welcomes all – local students have taken to it big time. No alcohol. (www.mosquekitchen.com; 31 Nicolson Sq; mains £5-7; ☉11am-8pm; 🖉👪; ☐all South Bridge buses)

Surgeons' Hall Museums (p164)

ROMAN BABAKIN/SHUTTERSTOCK ©

Food Festival

The four-day **Edinburgh Food Festival** (www.edfoodfest.com; George Sq Gdns, EH8 9JZ; ⏰ Jul), based in George Square Gardens, precedes the opening of the Edinburgh Fringe with a packed programme of talks, cookery demonstrations, tastings, food stalls and entertainment.

Drinking

Bennet's Bar   PUB

19 🔵 MAP P162, D3

Situated beside the King's Theatre (p172), Bennet's (established in 1839) has managed to hang on to almost all of its beautiful Victorian fittings, from the stained-glass windows and the ornate mirrors to the wooden gantry and the brass water taps on the bar (for your whisky – there are over 100 from which to choose). (📞 0131-229 5143; www.kilderkingroup.co.uk/bennets; 8 Leven St; ⏰ 11am-1am; 🚌 all Tollcross buses)

Royal Dick   MICROBREWERY

Located in Summerhall (see 2 👁 Map p162, H4) the decor at the Royal Dick alludes to its past as the home of Edinburgh University's veterinary school: there are shelves of laboratory glassware and walls covered with animal bones, even an old operating ta-

ble. But rather than being creepy, it's a warm, welcoming place for a drink, serving artisan ales and craft gins produced by its own microbrewery and distillery. (📞 0131-560 1572; www.summerhall. co.uk/the-royal-dick; 1 Summerhall; ⏰ 2-10pm; 🚭; 🚌 41, 42)

Brauhaus   BAR

20 🔵 MAP P162, D2

This bar is fairly small – half a dozen bar stools, a couple of sofas and a scattering of seats – but its ambition is huge, with a vast menu of bottled beers from all over the world, ranging from the usual suspects (Belgium, Germany and the Czech Republic) to more unusual brews and more than 60 single-malt whiskies. (📞 0131-447 7721; 105 Lauriston Pl; ⏰ 5pm-1am Sun-Fri, 3pm-1am Sat; 🚭; 🚌 23, 27, 45, 47)

Auld Hoose   PUB

21 🔵 MAP P162, H3

Promoting itself as the Southside's only 'alternative' pub, the Auld Hoose certainly lives up to its reputation, with unpretentious decor, a jukebox, gig posters on the walls, a range of real ales from remote Scottish microbreweries and a regular quiz night (8pm Tuesdays). There's good grub too. (📞 0131-668 2934; www.theauldhoose. co.uk; 23-25 St Leonards St; ⏰ noon-12.45am Mon-Sat, 12.30pm-12.45am Sun; 🚭🐾; 🚌 14)

Pear Tree House

PUB

22 MAP P162, G2

Set in an 18th-century house with a cobbled courtyard, the Pear Tree is a student favourite, with an open fire in winter, bright modern decor and the city's biggest and most popular beer garden in summer. (☎0131-667 7533; www.peartreeedinburgh.co.uk; 38 W Nicolson St, EH8 9DD; ⏰11am-1am; 📶; 🚌2, 41, 42, 47)

Cloisters

PUB

23 MAP P162, D3

Housed in a converted manse (minister's house) that once belonged to the next-door church, and furnished with well-worn, mismatched wooden tables and chairs, Cloisters now ministers to a mixed congregation of students, locals and real-ale connoisseurs. It has decent food and coffee, and a nice warm fireplace in winter. (☎0131-221 9997; www.cloistersbar.com; 26 Brougham St; ⏰noon-midnight Mon-Thu, to 1am Fri & Sat, 12.30pm-midnight Sun; 🚌24)

Caley Sample Room

PUB

24 MAP P162, A3

The Sample Room is a big, lively, convivial pub serving a wide range of wines and excellent real ales, and some of the best pub grub in the city (brunch is served 10am to 3pm at weekends). It's popular with sports fans, too, who gather to watch football and rugby matches on the large-screen TVs. (☎0131-337 7204; www.thecaley sampleroom.co.uk; 58 Angle Park Tce; ⏰noon-midnight Mon-Thu, to 1am Fri, 10am-1am Sat, 10am-midnight Sun; 📶 ♿; 🚌4, 34, 35, 44, 300)

Canny Man's

PUB

25 MAP P162, C6

A lovably eccentric pub, the Canny Man's consists of a crowded warren of tiny rooms crammed with a bizarre collection of antiques and curiosities (a description that could apply to some of the regulars). If you can get in, you'll find it serves excellent real ale, vintage port and Cuban cigars, and the best Bloody Marys in town. (☎0131-447 1484; www.cannymans.co.uk; 237 Morningside Rd; ⏰11am-11pm Sun-Wed, to midnight Thu & Sat, to 1am Fri; 📶; 🚌5, 11, 15, 16, 17, 23, 36)

Athletic Arms

PUB

26 MAP P162, A3

Nicknamed for the cemetery across the street – gravediggers used to nip in and slake their thirst here – the Diggers dates from 1897. It's still staunchly traditional – the decor has barely changed in 100 years – and is a beacon for real-ale drinkers, serving locally brewed 80-shilling ale. It's packed to the gills with football and rugby fans on match days. (Diggers; ☎0131-337 3822; www.athleticarms.com; 1-3 Angle Park Tce; ⏰11am-1am; 🐾; 🚌1, 34, 35)

Entertainment

Summerhall
THEATRE

Formerly Edinburgh University's veterinary school, the Summerhall (see 2 ⊙ Map p162, H4) complex is a major cultural centre and entertainment venue, with old halls and lecture theatres (including an original anatomy lecture theatre) now serving as venues for drama, dance, cinema and comedy. It's also one of the main venues for events during the **Edinburgh International Festival** (🎫0131-473 2000; www.eif.co.uk; ⏰Aug-Sep). (🎫0131-560 1580; www.summerhall. co.uk; 1 Summerhall; ⏰box office 10am-6pm; 🚌41, 42)

Cameo
CINEMA

27 ⭐ MAP P162, D3

The three-screen, independently owned Cameo is a good old-fashioned cinema (first opened in 1914) showing an imaginative mix of mainstream and art-house movies. There's a programme of late-night films and Sunday matinees, and the seats in screen 1 are big enough to get lost in. (🎫0871 902 5723; www.picturehouses.com/ cinema/Cameo_Picturehouse; 38 Home St; tickets £7.90-12.40; 📶; 🚌all Tollcross buses)

Edinburgh Festival Theatre
THEATRE

28 ⭐ MAP P162, G2

A beautifully restored art deco theatre with a modern all-glass frontage, the Festival is the city's main venue for opera, dance and ballet, but also stages musicals, concerts, drama and children's shows. (🎫0131-529 6000; www.capitaltheatres.com/festival; 13-29 Nicolson St; ⏰box office 10am-7.30pm; 🚌all South Bridge buses)

King's Theatre
THEATRE

29 ⭐ MAP P162, D3

The King's is a traditional theatre with a programme of musicals, drama, comedy and its famous Christmas pantomimes. (🎫0131-529 6000; www.capitaltheatres.com/ kings; 2 Leven St; ⏰box office 10am-6pm; 🚌all Tollcross buses)

The Union Canal

Built some 200 years ago and abandoned in the 1960s, the Union Canal was restored and reopened to navigation in 2002. Edinburgh Quays, its city-centre terminus in Tollcross, is a starting point for canal cruises, towpath walks and bike rides. The canal stretches west for 31 miles through the rural landscape of West Lothian to Falkirk, where it joins the Forth and Clyde Canal at the Falkirk Wheel boat lift. At Harrison Park, a mile southwest of Edinburgh Quays, is a pretty little canal basin with rowing boats for hire.

The Union Canal

Shopping

Lighthouse BOOKS

30  MAP P162, G2

Lighthouse is a radical independent bookshop that supports both small publishers and local writers. It stocks a wide range of political, gay and feminist literature, as well as non-mainstream fiction and nonfiction. (☎0131-662 9112; www.lighthousebookshop.com; 43 W Nicolson St; ⊗11am-6pm Mon-Sat, 11.30am-5pm Sun; ⛟41, 42)

Backbeat MUSIC

31  MAP P162, H3

If you're hunting for secondhand vinyl from way back, this cramped little shop has a stunning and constantly changing collection of jazz, blues, rock and soul, plus lots of '60s and '70s stuff. (☎0131-668 2666; 31 E Crosscauseway; ⊗10am-5.30pm Mon-Sat; ⛟all Newington buses)

Meadows Pottery CERAMICS

32  MAP P162, H4

This small shop sells a range of colourful, high-fired oxidised stoneware, both domestic and decorative, all hand thrown on the premises. If you can't find what you want, you can commission custom-made pieces. (☎0131-662 4064; www.themeadowspottery.com; 11a Summerhall Pl, EH9 1QE; ⊗10am-5pm Mon-Fri, to 4.30pm Sat; ⛟2, 41, 42)

Worth a Trip 🔭
Rosslyn Chapel

Many years may have passed since Dan Brown's novel The Da Vinci Code and the subsequent film came out, but floods of visitors still descend on Scotland's most beautiful and enigmatic church – Rosslyn Chapel. Built in the mid-15th century for Sir William St Clair, third prince of Orkney, its ornately carved interior is a monument to the mason's art.

Collegiate Church of St Matthew

www.rosslynchapel.com

Chapel Loan, Roslin

adult/child £9/free

🕐 9.30am-6pm Mon-Sat Jun-Aug, to 5pm Sep-May, noon-4.45pm Sun year-round

🚍 37

The Apprentice Pillar

The beautiful Apprentice Pillar is at the Lady Chapel's entrance. Four vines spiral around the pillar, issuing from eight dragons' mouths. At the top is an image of Isaac, son of Abraham, upon the altar.

Lucifer, the Fallen Angel

At head height in the Lady Chapel, to the left of the second window from the left, is a bound, upside-down angel, a symbol associated with Freemasonry. The arch is decorated with the Dance of Death.

The Green Man

On the boss at the base of the arch between the second and third windows from the left in the Lady Chapel is the Green Man (pictured). It's the finest example of 100-plus carvings of this pagan symbol of spring, fertility and rebirth.

Indian Corn?

The frieze around the south wall's second window is said to represent Indian corn (maize), but it predates Columbus' voyage to the New World. Other carvings resemble aloe vera, found in Africa and Asia.

The Apprentice

High in the southwestern corner, beneath an empty statue niche, is the head of the stonemason's apprentice. Apparently the Apprentice Pillar he created was so exquisitely carved that the mason jealously murdered him. The worn head on the side wall to the left is his grieving mother.

The Ceiling

The spectacular ceiling vault is decorated with engraved roses, lilies and stars; look for the sun and moon.

★ **Top Tips**

○ No photography or video is allowed inside the chapel.

○ It's worth buying the official guidebook by the Earl of Rosslyn (£5), finding a bench in the gardens and having a skim through before going into the chapel – the background information will make your visit all the more interesting.

✗ **Take a Break**

There's a **coffee shop** (Chapel Loan, Roslin, EH25 9PU; mains £5-10; 9.30am-6pm Mon-Sat Jun-Aug, to 5pm Sep-May, noon-4.45pm Sun year-round; 37) in the chapel's visitor centre, serving soup, sandwiches, coffee and cake, with a view over Roslin Glen.

★ **Getting There**

Lothian Bus 37 to Penicuik Deanburn links Edinburgh to the village of Roslin. (Bus 37 to Bush does not go via Roslin.)

Survival Guide

Before You Go   178
Book Your Stay 178
When to Go 178

Arriving in Edinburgh   179
Edinburgh Airport 179
Edinburgh Waverley Train Station 179

Getting Around   180
Bus 180
Tram 180
Taxi 180
Bike 181
Car & Motorcycle 181

Essential Information   181
Accessible Travel 181
Business Hours 182
Discount Cards 182
Electricity 182
Money 182
Public Holidays 183
Safe Travel 183
Telephone Services 183
Toilets 184
Tourist Information 184
Visas 184

Grassmarket (p53) JEFF WHYTE/SHUTTERSTOCK ©

Before You Go

Book Your Stay

○ Hotels and hostels are found throughout the Old and New Towns; midrange B&Bs and guesthouses are concentrated outside the centre in the suburbs of Tollcross, Bruntsfield, Newington and Pilrig.

○ If you're driving, don't even think about staying in the city centre unless your hotel has its own private car park – parking in the centre is a nightmare.

○ Edinburgh is packed to the gills during the festival period (August) and over Hogmanay (New Year). If you want a room during these periods, book as far in advance as you can – a year ahead if possible.

○ It's best to book at least a few months ahead for accommodation at Easter and from mid-May to mid-September.

○ Edinburgh accommodation costs: budget is less than £65, midrange

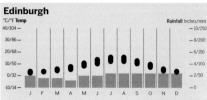

Edinburgh

When to Go

○ **Winter** (Dec–Feb) Cold and dark with occasional snow; Christmas decorations; Hogmanay and Burns Night celebrations.

○ **Spring** (Mar–May) Cold to mild, damp, occasional sun; flowers and blossom everywhere.

○ **Summer** (Jun–Aug) Mild to warm but occasionally wet; main tourist season; city packed out for festival in August.

○ **Autumn** (Sep–Nov) Mild to chilly, often damp; autumn colours in parks; tourist crowds have left.

is £65 to £130, and top end is more than £130, based on the cost of a double room with breakfast.

○ If you're staying for a week or more, a short-term or serviced apartment might be more economical.

○ If you arrive in Edinburgh without a place to stay, the booking service at the **Edinburgh tourist office** (Edinburgh iCentre; ☏ 0131-473 3820; www.visitscotland.com/info/services/edinburgh-icentre-p234441; 249 High St, Royal Mile; ⏰ 10am-4.30pm Mon-Sat, to 4pm Sun Oct-Mar, longer hours Apr-Sep; 🛜; 🚌 23, 27, 41, 42) will try to find you a room to suit you (and will charge a £5 fee if successful). If you have the time, pick up the tourist office's accommodation brochure and ring around yourself.

Useful Websites

VisitScotland (www.visitscotland.com/edinburgh) Wide range of options from the official website.

Lonely Planet (lonely
planet.com/scotland/
edinburgh/hotels)
Recommendations and
bookings.

This Is Edinburgh
(www.edinburgh.org)
Promotional website
with lots of accommo-
dation and weekend-
break offers.

Best Budget

Code – The Court
(www.codehostels.
com) Stylish, modern
hostel in a former Old
Town prison.

**Edinburgh Central
Youth Hostel** (www.
hostellingscotland.
org.uk) Hostelling
Scotland's five-star
establishment close to
the city centre.

Safestay Edinburgh
(www.safestay.com)
A big, bright, modern
hostel in the heart of
the Old Town.

Best Midrange

**Sheridan Guest
House** (www.sheridan
edinburgh.com) A little
haven hidden away to
the north of the New
Town.

94DR (www.94dr.com)
Gorgeous boutique

B&B in a sensitively
restored Victorian
town house.

14 Hart Street
(www.14hartstreet.
co.uk) Elegant quar-
ters nestled close to
the bars and restau-
rants of Broughton St.

Best Top End

House of Gods (www.
houseofgodshotel.
com) Decadently over-
the-top boutique hotel.

**Southside Guest
House** (www.south
sideguesthouse.co.uk)
South Edinburgh town
house that feels more
like an upmarket hotel.

**Witchery by the Cas-
tle** (www.thewitchery.
com) Nine lavish
Gothic suites in the
shadow of Edinburgh
Castle.

Arriving in
Edinburgh

Edinburgh
Airport

Edinburgh Airport
(EDI; ☎ 0844 448 8833;
www.edinburghairport.
com) Airlink 100 bus

runs from the airport
to South St David
St, at the east end of
Princes St (one way/
return £4.50/7.50,
30 minutes), near the
main train station,
via Haymarket and
the West End every
12 minutes from 4am
to 1am and every 30
minutes through the
night. Trams run from
the airport to the city
centre (one way/return
£6.50/9, 33 minutes,
every six to eight
minutes from 6.15am
to 10.45pm). An airport
taxi to the city centre
costs around £20
and takes 20 to 30
minutes.

Edinburgh
Waverley Train
Station

**Edinburgh Waverley
Train Station** The
main train station is
Edinburgh Waverley,
located in the heart
of the city between
the Old Town and New
Town. Trains arriving
from and departing for
the west also stop at
Edinburgh Haymarket
station, which is more
convenient for the
West End.

Bus Info On Your Phone

Transport for Edinburgh has created free smartphone apps (www.tfeapp.com) that provide route maps, timetables and live waiting times for city buses and trams. The companion m-tickets app allows you to buy bus and tram tickets on your phone (minimum purchase is £4).

Getting Around

Bus

○ Bus timetables, route maps and fare guides are posted at all main bus and tram stops, and you can pick up a copy of the free *Lothian Buses Route Map* from **Lothian Buses Travel-hub** (31 Waverley Bridge, EH1 1BQ; ⏰9am-5pm Mon-Sat; 🚌all Princes St buses).

○ Adult fares within the city are £1.80; purchase from the bus driver. Children aged under five travel free and those aged five to 15 pay a flat fare of 90p.

○ On Lothian Buses you must pay the driver the exact fare, but First buses will give change.

Lothian Bus drivers also sell a day ticket (£4.50) that gives unlimited travel on Lothian buses and trams (within the City Zone, ie not including the airport) for a day; a family day ticket (up to two adults and three children) costs £9.50.

○ Night-service buses, which run hourly between midnight and 5am, charge a flat fare of £3.

○ You can also buy a Ridacard (from Travelshops; not available from bus drivers) that gives unlimited travel for one week for £20.

○ Lost-property enquiries should be made online (www.lothianbuses.com/lost-property).

Tram

○ Edinburgh's tram system (www.edinburghtrams.com) consists of one line from Edinburgh Airport to York Pl, at the top of Leith Walk, via Haymarket, the West End and Princes St.

○ Tickets are integrated with the city's Lothian Buses, costing £1.80 for a single journey within the city boundary, or £6.50 to the airport.

○ Trams run every 10 minutes Monday to Saturday and every 12 to 15 minutes on Sunday, from 5.30am to 11pm.

Taxi

○ Edinburgh's black taxis can be hailed in the street, ordered by phone (extra 80p charge) or picked up at one of the many central ranks.

○ The minimum charge is £3 (£4 at night) for the first 450m, then 25p for every subsequent 168m – a typical 2-mile trip across the city centre will cost around £6 to £7.

○ Tipping is up to you – because of the high fares, local people rarely tip on short journeys, but they occasionally round up to the nearest 50p on longer ones.

Central Taxis (☏ 0131-229 2468; www.taxis-edinburgh.co.uk)

City Cabs (☏ 0131-228 1211; www.citycabs.co.uk)

Bike

○ Edinburgh is well equipped with bike lanes and dedicated cycle tracks.

○ You can buy a map of the city's cycle routes from most bike shops.

○ **Biketrax** (☏ 0131-228 6633; www.biketrax.co.uk; 11-13 Lochrin Pl, EH3 9QX; hybrid/e-bike per day from £25/48; ⏲ 9.30am-6pm Mon-Fri, to 5.30pm Sat, noon-5pm Sun, longer hours Apr-Sep; 🚌 all Tollcross buses) rents out mountain bikes, hybrid bikes, road bikes, Brompton folding bikes and electric bikes. You'll need a debit- or credit-card deposit and photo ID.

Car & Motorcycle

○ Though useful for day trips beyond the city, a car in central Edinburgh is more of a liability than a convenience.

○ There's no parking on main roads into the city from 7.30am to 6.30pm Monday to Saturday.

Also, parking in the city centre can be a nightmare.

○ On-street parking is controlled by self-service ticket machines from 8.30am to 6.30pm Monday to Saturday, and costs from £2.40 to £4.90 per hour, with a 30-minute to four-hour maximum.

○ All the big international car-rental agencies have offices in Edinburgh, including **Avis** (☏ 0344-544 6059; www.avis.co.uk; 24 E London St; ⏲ 8am-6pm Mon-Fri, to 3pm Sat, 10am-2pm Sun; 🚌 10,11) and **Europcar** (☏ 0371-384 3453; www.europcar.co.uk; Platform 2, Waverley Station; ⏲ 7am-5pm; 🚌 all Princes St buses).

Essential Information

Accessible Travel

○ Download Lonely Planet's free Accessible Travel guides from https://shop.lonely-planet.com/categories/accessible-travel.

○ Edinburgh's Old Town, with its steep hills, narrow closes, flights of stairs and cobbled streets, is a challenge for wheelchair users.

○ Large new hotels and modern tourist attractions are usually accessible; however, many B&Bs and guesthouses are in hard-to-adapt older buildings that lack ramps and lifts.

○ Newer buses have steps or kneeling

Emergency & Useful Phone Numbers

UK's country code	☏ 44
International access code	☏ 00
Police (emergency)	☏ 999 or 112
Police (non-emergency)	☏ 101
Fire	☏ 999 or 112
Ambulance	☏ 999 or 112

suspension that lowers for access, but it's wise to check before setting out. Most black taxis are wheelchair-friendly.

○ Many banks are fitted with induction loops to assist the hearing impaired. Some attractions have Braille guides for the visually impaired.

○ **VisitScotland** (www.visitscotland.com/accommodation/accessible) has an online guide to accessible accommodation for travellers with disabilities.

Business Hours

Banks 9.30am–4pm Monday to Friday; some branches open 9.30am–1pm Saturday

Businesses 9am–5pm Monday to Friday

Pubs and Bars 11am–11pm Monday to Thursday, to 1am Friday and Saturday, 12.30pm–11pm Sunday

Restaurants noon–2.30pm and 6pm–10pm

Shops 9am–5.30pm Monday to Saturday (some to 8pm Thursday), 11am–5pm Sunday

Discount Cards

○ If you plan to visit the Royal Yacht *Britannia* as well as Edinburgh Castle and the Palace of Holyroodhouse, consider buying a **Royal Edinburgh Ticket** (www.edinburghtour.com/royal-edinburgh-ticket), which includes admission to all three, plus unlimited travel on hop-on, hop-off tour buses among the various attractions.

Electricity

Type G
230V/50Hz

Money
ATMs

○ Automatic teller machines (ATMs – often

called cashpoints) are widespread.

○ You can use Visa, MasterCard, Amex, Cirrus, Plus and Maestro cards to withdraw cash from ATMs belonging to most banks and building societies.

○ Cash withdrawals from non-bank ATMs, usually found in shops, may be subject to a charge of up to £2.

Currency

○ The unit of currency in the UK is the pound sterling (£).

○ One pound sterling consists of 100 pence (called 'p' colloquially).

○ Banknotes come in denominations of £5, £10, £20 and £50.

○ Scottish banks issue their own banknotes, meaning there's quite a variety of different notes in circulation. They are harder to exchange outside the UK, so swap for Bank of England notes before you leave.

Money Changing

○ The best-value places to change money are post offices, where no commission is charged.

○ Be careful using

bureaux de change; they may offer good exchange rates but frequently levy outrageous commissions and fees.

Tipping

Hotels One pound per bag is standard; gratuities for cleaning staff are completely at your discretion.

Pubs Tips are not expected unless table service is provided, then tip £1 for a round of drinks.

Restaurants For decent service tip 10% and up to 15% at more expensive places. Check to see if service has been added to the bill already (most likely for large groups).

Taxis Not for short journeys; you can round up to the nearest 50p on longer ones.

Public Holidays

New Year's Day 1 January

New Year Bank Holiday 2 January

Spring Bank Holiday Second Monday in April

Good Friday Friday before Easter Sunday

Easter Monday Mon-

Phone Codes & Rates

International access code	☏00
Edinburgh area code	☏0131
Mobile phone numbers	☏07xxx; 10p to 20p per minute from landlines, 3p to 55p per minute from mobiles
Local calls	☏0845; up to 7p per minute from landlines & mobiles, plus access charge
National calls	☏0870; up to 13p per minute from landlines & mobiles, plus access charge
Premium calls	☏09; up to £3.60 per minute from landlines & mobiles, plus access charge, plus 5p to £6 per call
Toll-free numbers	☏0800 or 0808; free from UK landlines & mobiles

day following Easter Sunday

May Day First Monday in May

Christmas Day 25 December

Boxing Day 26 December

Safe Travel

○ Lothian Rd, Dalry Rd, Rose St and the western end of Princes St, at the junction with Shandwick Pl and Queensferry St, can get a bit rowdy late on Friday and Saturday nights after pub-closing time.

○ Calton Hill offers good views during the day but is best avoided at night.

○ Be aware that the area between Salamander St and Leith Links in Leith is a red-light district – lone women here at any time of day might be approached by kerb crawlers.

Telephone Services

○ There are plenty of public phones in Edinburgh, operated by coins, phonecards or credit cards; phonecards are available in newsagents.

o Edinburgh's area code is 0131, followed by a seven-digit number. You only need to dial the 0131 prefix when you are calling Edinburgh from outside the city, or if you're dialling from a mobile.

o To call overseas from the UK, dial the international access code (00), then the area code (dropping any initial 0), followed by the telephone number.

Mobile Phones

o The UK uses the GSM 900/1800 network, which is compatible with the rest of Europe, Australia and New Zealand, but not with the North American GSM 1900 system or Japanese mobile technology.

o If in doubt, check with your service provider; some North Americans have GSM 1900/900 phones that will work in the UK.

o Edinburgh has excel-lent 4G coverage but, as of 2020, only patchy 5G.

Toilets

o Public toilets are most-ly free to use and are spread (thinly) across the city.

o Most are open from 9am to 4pm, up to 8pm in summer.

o Find more info at www.edinburgh.gov.uk; search for 'public toilet'.

Tourist Information

o **Edinburgh Tourist Office** (Edinburgh iCentre; ☎0131-473 3820; www.visitscotland.com/info/services/edinburgh-icentre-p234441; 249 High St, Royal Mile; ☺10am-4.30pm Mon-Sat, to 4pm Sun Oct-Mar, longer hours Apr-Sep; ☎: ☐23, 27, 41, 42) Accommodation-booking service, currency exchange, gift shop and bookshop, internet access, and counters selling tickets for Edinburgh city tours and Scottish Citylink bus services.

Visas

o If you're a citizen of the EEA (European Economic Area) nations or Switzerland you don't need a visa to enter or work in Britain.

o You will not be able to use your EEA or Swiss national ID card to enter the UK from 1 October 2021, unless you have settled status.

o Visa regulations are al-ways subject to change, which is especially likely after Britain's exit from the EU from 1 January 2021, so it's essential to check the latest before leaving home.

o At the time of research, if you're a citizen of Australia, Canada, New Zealand, Japan, Israel, the US and several other countries, you can stay for up to six months (no visa required) but are not allowed to work.

o Nationals of many countries, including South Africa, will need to obtain a visa: for more info see www.gov.uk/check-uk-visa.

Behind the Scenes

Send Us Your Feedback

We love to hear from travellers – your comments help make our books better. We read every word, and we guarantee that your feedback goes straight to the authors. Visit **lonelyplanet.com/contact** to submit your updates and suggestions.

Note: We may edit, reproduce and incorporate your comments in Lonely Planet products such as guidebooks, websites and digital products, so let us know if you don't want your comments reproduced or your name acknowledged. For a copy of our privacy policy visit lonelyplanet.com/privacy.

Neil's Thanks

Thanks to the friendly and helpful Edinburgh tourist office staff; to Dona Milne and Alastair Short; to Brendan Bolland, Jenny Neil, Tom and Christine Duffin, and Steve Hall; and, as ever, to Carol Downie. Thanks also to Sandie Kestell and the rest of the editorial team at Lonely Planet.

Acknowledgements

Cover photograph: Calton Hill, Westend61/Getty Images©

This Book

This 6th edition of Lonely Planet's *Pocket Edinburgh* guidebook was researched and written by Neil Wilson. The previous two editions were also written by Neil. This guidebook was produced by the following:

Senior Product Editor Sandie Kestell

Senior Cartographer Alison Lyall

Product Editor Fergus O'Shea

Book Designer Catalina Aragón

Assisting Editors Nigel Chin, Maja Vatrić, Brana Vladisavljevic

Assisting Cartographer Mark Griffiths

Cover Researcher Fergal Condon

Thanks to Genna Patterson

Index

See also separate subindexes for:

⊗ **Eating p188**

◉ **Drinking p189**

✪ **Entertainment p190**

🔒 **Shopping p190**

A

accessible travel 181-2
accommodation 178-9
activities 31, *see also individual activities*
Adam, Robert 26, 102, 105, 106, 135
airport 179
ambulance 181
Animal World 49
Apprentice Pillar 175
architecture 26-7
area codes 183
art 72
Arthur's Seat 85, 86, 82
Arthur's Seat area, *see* Holyrood
ATMs 182

B

bars 14-15, *see also* Drinking *subindex*
bathrooms 184
beer 15
Beltane 25
bicycle travel 181
Biscuit Factory 152

Sights **000**
Map Pages **000**

Blackford Hill 166
boat cruises 172
boat tours 30
body snatchers 51, 61
book sculptures 87
books 19, 114
Broughton 111
budget 34
Burke, William 61
Burns, Robert 23, 59, 61
bus tours 30, 151
bus travel 180
business hours 14, 182
Bute House 102

C

Calm on Canning Street 123
Calton Hill 103
Camera Obscura & World of Illusions 58-9
Canongate Kirkyard 61-2
car travel 181
Castle Esplanade 43
cell phones 34, 184
Charlotte Square 102
children, travel with 29
churches 58, 60, 61, 86, 95, 174-5
City Art Centre 62-3
climate 178

clubs, *see* Drinking, Entertainment *subindexes*
Cockburn St 75
cocktails 15
Collective/City Observatory 103
costs 34
Cowgate 53
Craigmillar Castle 165-6
Cramond 157
cullen skink 12-13
currency 34, 182
cycling 181

D

dangers 183
Dean Bridge 123
Dean Village 123
Dean Village area, *see* West End
disabilities, travellers with 181-2
Dovecot Studios 62
Dr Neil's Garden 85
drinking 14-17, *see also* Drinking *subindex, individual neighbourhoods*
Duddingston Kirk 86-7
Duddingston Village 83
Dundas House 104

E

eating 10-13, *see also* Eating *subindex, individual neighbourhoods*
Edinburgh Castle 42-5, 55, 44
Edinburgh Festival Fringe 25
Edinburgh Food Festival 170
Edinburgh International Festival 25
Edinburgh Printmakers' Workshop & Gallery 164-5
Edinburgh Sculpture Workshop 151
Edinburgh Zoo 105
electricity 182
emergencies 181
entertainment, *see* Entertainment *subindex, individual neighbourhoods*
events 24-5

F

Farmers Market 127
festivals 24-5
fire 181
Floatarium Spa 139

Flodden Wall 53
Floral Clock 95

G

galleries 22-3
gay travellers 111
**General Register
House** 105
**George Heriot's
School** 53
George IV Bridge 66
Georgian House 102
ghost tours 60
Gilmerton Cove 164
Gladstone's Land 59
Grassmarket 53
Great Gallery 79
**Greyfriars Bobby
Statue** 61
Greyfriars Kirk 60
Greyfriars Kirkyard
53, 60-1

H

haggis 10
Hare, William 61
Heriot Row 97
**Hermitage
House** 166
**Hermitage of
Braid** 166
highlights 6-9
hiking 86, 157, see
also walking tours
history 106
Hogmanay 25
holidays 183
Holyrood 77-89, **84**
drinking 88-9
food 87-8
itineraries 82-3, **82**
sights 78-81, 85-7
transport 77
walks 82-3, **82**
Holyrood Abbey 79

**Holyrood
Distillery** 87
Holyrood Park 86
**Honours of
Scotland** 45
Hutton's Section 83

I

itineraries 32-3, see
also individual
neighbourhoods

J

Jacob's Ladder 83
jewellery 19
**John Hope
Gateway** 135
**John Knox
House** 60

L

language 34
Leith 147-59, **150**
drinking 157-8
food 152-6
shopping 158-9
sights 148-9, 151-2
transport 147
walks 157
Leith Links 151
lesbian travellers 111
literature 114
live music venues,
see Entertainment
subindex

M

markets 19, 127
Mary, Queen of
Scots 79
McCall Smith,
Alexander 114
McWilliam, Candia 114
Meadows, The 165
Melville Monument

97, 104
**Millennium Clock
Tower** 49
miniature coffins 88
mobile phones 34, 184
money 34, 182-3
money changing 182-3
Mons Meg 44
monuments 27
motorcycle travel 181
**Museum of
Edinburgh** 55, 58
museums 22-3
music 68, see also
Entertainment
subindex

N

**National
Monument** 104
**National Museum of
Scotland** 48-51
Nelson Monument
103-4
New Town 91-117,
100-1
drinking 111-13
entertainment 113
food 105-11
history 106
itineraries 96-7,
98-9, **96**, **98**
shopping 115-17
sights 92-5, 102-5
transport 91
walks 96-7, 98-9,
96, **98**
Newhaven 152
nightlife 14-15, see
also Drinking,
Entertainment
subindexes

O

Old Calton Burial
Ground 104

Old Town 41-75, **56-7**
drinking 68-71
entertainment 71-3
food 63-8
history 64
itineraries 52-5,
52, **54**
shopping 73-5
sights 42-55, 58-62
transport 41
walks 52-5, **52**, **54**
One O'Clock Gun
43, 108
opening hours 14, 182
**Our Dynamic
Earth** 86
**Out of the Blue Drill
Hall** 152

P

**Palace of
Holyroodhouse**
55, 78-9
parks 94-5, 134-5
Parliament Hall 63
Pentland Hills 166
People's Story 60
police 181
Princes Street 18
**Princes Street
Gardens** 94-5
**Prisons of War
Exhibition** 44
public holidays 183
pubs 14-15, see also
Drinking subindex

Q

Queen's Drive 83
Queen's Gallery 86

R

Radical Road 83
Raeburn
Place** 137

Rankin, Ian 88, 97, 112, 114

Real Mary King's Close 46-7, 55

restaurants 10-11, *see also* Eating subindex

resurrection men 51, 61

Ross Bandstand 95

Rosslyn Chapel 174-5

Royal Botanic Garden 134-5

Royal Mile 64

Royal Scottish Academy 102

Royal Yacht Britannia 148-9

S

safety 183

Scotch Whisky Experience 55, 58

Scotsman Steps 72

Scott Monument 95

Scottish National Gallery 102

Scottish National Gallery of Modern Art 120-1

Scottish National Portrait Gallery 92-3

Scottish Parliament Building 55, 80-1

Scottish Poetry Library 87

seafood 11, 152

shopping 18-21, *see also* Shopping subindex, individual neighbourhoods

Sights 000
Map Pages **000**

Shore, the 151

South Bridge 66

South Bridge Vaults 53

South Edinburgh 161-73, **162-3**

entertainment 172-3

food 166-9

shopping 173

sights 164-6

transport 161

walks 166

souvenirs 20-1

Spark, Muriel 114

St Andrew Square 104

St Andrew's House 105

St Anthony's Chapel 83

St Bernard's Well 139

St Cuthbert's Parish Church 95

St Giles Cathedral 55, 58, 68

St John's Church 95

St Margaret's Loch 83

St Margaret's Well 83

St Stephen Street 137

Stevenson, Robert Louis 59, 97, 114

Stockbridge 133-45, **138**

drinking 141-3

food 139-41

itineraries 136-7, **136**

shopping 143-5

sights 134-5, 139

transport 133

walks 136-7, **136**

Summerhall 164

Surgeons' Hall Museums 164

T

taxis 180-1

telephone services 34, 183-4

tenements 64

time 34

tipping 34, 183

toilets 184

tourist information 184

tours 30

train station 179

trams 180

transport 35, 179-81

Trinity House 151-2

U

underground vaults 66

Union Canal 172

V

vegetarian travellers 11

Victoria Terrace 53

viewpoints 28

visas 34, 184

W

walking tours 30

Holyrood & Arthur's Seat 82-3, **82**

New Town 96-7, 98-9, **96**, **98**

Old Town 52-3, 54-5, **52**, **54**

Stockbridge 136-7, **136**

Water of Leith 124, 140

weather 178

websites 178-9

Welsh, Irvine 114

West End 119-31, **122**

drinking 127-8

entertainment 128-30

food 123-7

shopping 130-1

sights 120-1, 123

transport 119

whisky bars 15, *see also* Drinking *subindex*

writers 59, 88, 97, 112, 114

Writers' Museum 55, 59

Z

zoos 105

⊗ **Eating**

A

Amber 13, 67

B

Baba 105-6

Bell's Diner 140

Bon Vivant 109

Bross Bagels 156

Buffalo Grill 168

C

Café at the Palace 79

Cafe Milk 126

Cafe Modern One 121

Cafe Portrait 93

Cafe St Honore 109

Cannonball Restaurant 63

Chop House Leith 155-6

Condita 166

Contini 109

D

David Bann 67
Dishoom 107
Dome 108-9

E

Edinburgh Food
    Studio 167
Edinburgh Larder 68
El Cartel 109-10

F

First Coast 167
Fishers Bistro 154
Fishmarket 153

G

Gardener's
    Cottage 106-7
Gateway
    Restaurant 137
Grain Store 65

H

Hideout Cafe 156
Holy Cow 110

I

Ivy on the Square 109

K

Kalpna 168
Kanpai Sushi 123
Kitchin 153

L

La P'tite Folie 125
Leith Farmers
    Market 156-7
Little Chartroom 154
Locanda de Gusti 167
Loudon's 168
Lovecrumbs 125-6

M

Maxie's Bistro 68
McKirdy's
    Steakhouse 124
Merienda 140-1
Mosque Kitchen
    169-70
Mums 63-5
Museum
    Brasserie 13

N

No 1 The Grange 13,
    167-8
Nok's Kitchen 140
Number One 108

O

Omar Khayyam 124
Ondine 63
Outlook 105

P

Pantry 140
Paolozzi's Kitchen 121
Paul Kitching 21212
    108
Pitt 155
Pizza Express 141

R

Rendezvous 126-7
Restaurant Martin
    Wishart 152-3
Rhubarb 87-8
Royal Deck Tea
    Room 149

S

Scottish Cafe &
    Restaurant 13, 110
Scott's Kitchen 66
Scran & Scallie 139
Shore 155

Söderberg (The
    Meadows) 168
Stack Dim Sum
    Bar 156

T

Taisteal 139
Terra Marique 124
Terrace Cafe 135
Timberyard 123
Time 4 Thai 111
Tuk Tuk 169
Twelve Triangles 154-5

U

Union Brew Lab 167
Urban Angel 107

V

Vesta Bar &
    Kitchen 125

W

Wedgwood 65
Westroom 124
White Horse Oyster &
    Seafood Bar 65
Wings 67-8
Witchery by the
    Castle 66

⊙ Drinking

A

Abbotsford 112
Antiquary 143
Artisan Roast 142-3
Athletic Arms 171-2
Auld Hoose 170

B

Bailie Bar 143
Bennet's Bar 170

Blue Blazer 127
Bongo Club 69
Bow Bar 68
Bramble 112
Brauhaus 170
BrewDog 69

C

Cabaret Voltaire 68-9
Café Royal Circle
    Bar 111
Cairngorm Coffee 128
Caley Sample
    Room 171
Canny Man's 171
Carriers
    Quarters 158
Cask & Barrel 113
CC Blooms 111
Checkpoint 69-70
Clark's Bar 112
Cloisters 171
Cumberland Bar
    112-13

E

Edinburgh Gin
    Distillery 128

G

Ghillie Dhu 128
Guildford Arms 112

H

Hemma 88
Holyrood 9A 70

I

Indigo Yard 127-8

J

Jolly Judge 70
Joseph Pearce's 111

K

Kay's Bar 142
Kilderkin 89

L

Last Word Saloon 141-2
Lioness of Leith 157
Liquid Room 70
Lucky Liquor Co 111

M

Malt Shovel 71
Mathers Bar 127

N

Nauticus 157
Nobles 158

O

Oxford Bar 112

P

Paradise Palms 70
Pear Tree House 171
Port O'Leith 158

R

Regent 89
Roseleaf 157
Royal Dick 170

S

Salt Horse Beer Shop
    & Bar 69
Sandy Bell's 70
Sheep Heid
    Inn 88-9
Stockbridge Tap 142

Sights 000
Map Pages **000**

T

Teuchters Landing 158
Tigerlily 113

V

Voyage of Buck 127

✪ Entertainment

Bannerman's 72
Bedlam Theatre 72-3
Cameo 172
Caves 71
Edinburgh Festival
    Theatre 172
Edinburgh Folk
    Club 113-15
Filmhouse 128
Henry's Cellar Bar
    128-9
Jazz Bar 72
King's Theatre 172-3
Murrayfield
    Stadium 130
Royal Lyceum
    Theatre 129
Royal Oak 71-2
Stand Comedy
    Club 113
Summerhall 172
Traverse Theatre 129
Usher Hall 129
Voodoo Rooms 113
Whistle Binkie's 72

🔒 Shopping

A

Adam Pottery 145
Alchemia 116
Annie Smith 144-5
Armstrong's 73
Assai Records 131

B

Backbeat 173
Bill Baber 73
Blackwell's Book-
    shop 74

C

Cookie 75
Curiouser and
    Curiouser 115

D

Dick's 144

F

Flux 158-9
Fopp 117

G

Galerie Mirages 145
Gallery 10 130
Geoffrey (Tailor) Inc 74
Ginger & Pickles 143-4
Godiva 73-4
Golden Hare Books 143

H

Hannah Zakari 73
Harvey Nichols 117

I

Ian Mellis 144

J

Jenners 117
John Lewis 117
Joyce Forsyth Designer
    Knitwear 74-5

K

Kilberry Bagpipes 75
Kinloch Anderson 158

L

Liam Ross 131
Life Story 115-16
Lighthouse 173
Lily Luna 130

M

McNaughton's
    Bookshop 116-17
Meadows Pottery 173
Miss Bizio 144
Mr Wood's Fossils 75
Museum Context 75

O

Ocean Terminal 159
One World Shop 117
Out of the Blue 159

P

Palenque 116
Perre 116
Pie in the Sky 75

R

Ragamuffin 73
Royal Mile Whiskies 73

S

Scottish Gallery 116
Sheila Fleet 144
Stockbridge Market
    143

U

Underground
    Solush'n 75

V

Valvona & Crolla 115

W

Wonderland 131